Colossal mist. P9-AFE-401
643.12 Smy 39092000589285

Silver City Public Library

CO[ ]S[ ]

MISTAKES

HOME SELLERS MAKE

and how to avoid them.

THE SIMPLE LANGUAGE GUIDE
TO HELP YOU SELL YOUR HOUSE FASTER AND
POCKET MORE MONEY.

Duncan Smythe

SILVER CITY PUBLIC LIBRARY
515 W. COLLEGE AVE.
SILVER CITY, NM 88061

643.12
Smy

0242325

$18   11/09

© 2008 Duncan Smythe
All Rights Reserved.

No part of this publication may be reproduced, stored in a retrieval system, or trans-
mitted, in any form or by any means, electronic, mechanical, photocopying, record-
ing, or otherwise, without the written permission of the author.

First published by Dog Ear Publishing
4010 W. 86th Street, Ste H
Indianapolis, IN 46268
www.dogearpublishing.net

ISBN: 978-159858-454-7

This book is printed on acid-free paper.

Printed in the United States of America

This book is dedicated
In Loving Memory
of Carol Lyons

She was my mentor and my inspiration
and one of the finest people I have ever known
The world is a lesser place without her

Acknowledgements

Many thanks to Kirk Kinkade, Mary Olive Stone,
Sam Stone, Nancy Humphrey and Jane Patricco
without whose proofreading skills this book
would have been incomprehensible.

Thank you to Madeline Sollaccio for
her always interesting and frequently
outrageous real estate stories.

A special thank you to fellow Broker Lou Faruolo,
whose real estate expertise made this book far
more accurate and informative.

Attention Realtors

If you have interesting, unusual or humorous
real estate stories you would like to share in a book,
please e-mail them to me: stories@colossalmistakes.com

Introduction

A wise person once told me that the stress of moving takes a year off your life. I don't doubt it. The prospect of selling your house and buying another one, packing up all your stuff, transporting it and then unpacking everything in a new location is harrowing. A hundred times I've heard people say "I'm never moving again". Selling your house is definitely a high-stress undertaking.

On my first day selling real estate I was just getting settled in my new office when I heard my first story of a home sale disaster. The seller had made a mistake which had resulted in an excellent deal on their house falling apart. It was completely avoidable. Since then I've heard thousands of similar stories, from old-time Realtors, brand new agents, and everyone in between.

Helping you to avoid mistakes, minor or colossal, is my mission. What you read here can save you time, anxiety and (most importantly) a lot of money. Selling a house is a very complicated and detail-filled transaction. I want to help you do it right, but most of all I want to help you steer clear of the errors, omissions and harmful mistakes I have seen home sellers make.

It has been my experience that the two most important things to a home seller are getting the best price for the house and selling quickly. I have included many tips and suggestions to facilitate a faster sale and show you how to prepare and market your house to get the best price.

This book is a terrific first step in your planning process if you want to do it the right way.

Good Luck!

Author's Note – *The word Realtor is capitalized throughout this book because it is a title which is trademarked. It is used only by members of the National Association of Realtors. Not all real estate agents are Realtors.*

Contents

GETTING STARTED

A smooth move
starts with a plan

Where do I start?

If you've never sold a house before, hang on, it can be a very bumpy ride. If you thought *buying* a house was a pain - get ready, selling can be a lot worse. A home sale rarely proceeds without glitches. With the proper planning and preparation, you can minimize the problems and stress.

Try to remember what the search process was like when you bought the house you're living in now: Rushing to see a new listing; Canceling an appointment at the last minute; Walking through a house you really hated while telling the owners how nice it was; Spending weeks or months searching and thinking that you would never find a house you really liked. Sound familiar?

Now you're on the other end of all that aggravation. You've decided to sell your house.

Ask yourself WHY?

That's right. Ask yourself why you are selling your house. It is a fundamental and important question. Is your motivation based on *want* or is it based on *need*? Knowing why you are selling will help you focus on the level of urgency for your sale.

Your motivation for selling your house is a consideration in determining how it should be marketed. When it should be put on the market, how quickly it will sell, how much you will get for it, and possibly who will buy it may all depend on your motivation. Knowing your own motivation helps you develop a strategy to successfully sell your home quickly for the best possible price.

Scratching your head? There are many reasons for selling your house. Here are just a few:

REASON #1:

"We've outgrown it"

We need more bedrooms.

We want a larger kitchen.

We must have a two-car garage.

The yard is just too small.

My wife needs an in-home office.

The dogs need room to run.

We want a basement.

LEVEL OF URGENCY - MEDIUM

Moving up to a larger house is a very common situation, which every family has to deal with at least once. Nearly everyone outgrows their house. If you have a plan, this should not be a high pressure circumstance. If, on the other hand, you've waited until you're seven months pregnant and you find yourself saying *"Oh my God, where will we put the baby?"*, then, of course, the situation has become a bit more urgent.

REASON #2:

"The community is changing"

All the old neighbors have moved away, and it's just not the same.

We want a better school system.

Housing values have decreased.

We're afraid if we stay any longer, we'll really lose money on our investment.

LEVEL OF URGENCY - VARIES

In this case, you are usually under no immediate pressure to move, but if your surroundings are in decline, selling your home may present unique challenges. The house could take much longer to sell than it would in another area. Pricing is always important, but in this particular case it becomes even more critical.

REASON #3:

"We make more money and want something better"

> *Now that we're moving up financially, we want to move to a more upscale neighborhood or to another town.*

LEVEL OF URGENCY - LOW

Again, there is no immediate pressure. You have plenty of time to prepare the house for sale to maximize the return on your investment and find the house of your dreams.

REASON #4:

"Job transfer"

> *We have to sell, I have been transferred.*

LEVEL OF URGENCY - HIGH

This presents a situation where there is pressure to sell and move because of a deadline. There is high motivation to sell the house quickly. When you are in a hurry, underpricing for a quicker sale may be a reasonable course of action, but you don't want to give the house away. You will still get a check at the closing, it just may not be as large as it could be.

REASON #5:

"We don't need this much room anymore"

The kids have grown up and gone.

The two of us don't need all these bedrooms.

Why pay property tax on space we don't use?

LEVEL OF URGENCY - LOW

Empty nesters are a rapidly growing segment of our population. Baby boomers are reaching retirement age. When kids have moved out, there may not be a reason to stay in the family home any more. It may seem that it just doesn't make sense to continue maintaining a house with space you don't need. In this circumstance, there usually is not a lot of pressure to sell, but there is concern over finding just the right place to live. This may be the last time you move, so you want to get it right.

REASON #6:

"We found our dream house"

We found exactly what we wanted, so we bought it and now we have to sell ours.

LEVEL OF URGENCY - HIGH

Purchasing another house is a great motivator. You know you have to sell your current house because you plan to use the proceeds from the sale to buy the new house. It does create a certain level of anxiety knowing that you must sell the house because you are faced with a deadline.

REASON #7:

"We bought a house in Florida for retirement"

We plan to move there eventually. We just want to get the best price for this house.

LEVEL OF URGENCY - LOW

A lower level of motivation here. Not in a big rush, but you do want to sell and close on your existing home sometime in the foreseeable future. To help with your planning, it's best to set a timetable for your move.

REASON #8:

"My Uncle Harry passed away and left the house to me"

I just have to sell it.

LEVEL OF URGENCY - HIGH

Selling the house of someone who is deceased is called an estate sale. Clearing the legal hurdles before the house can be listed for sale will take some time, typically six to twelve months.

Sometimes, the most challenging task in an estate sale is distributing the belongings of the deceased. This can take a long time depending on the number of heirs to the estate. It is not uncommon among heirs to have disagreements over personal property. Cleaning out the house can be not just time-consuming, but emotionally draining as well. For planning purposes, you'll want to ask your attorney how long the probate process may take.

Have you determined your motivation?

There are many reasons to sell a house and the motivation is different for each reason. Knowing your motivation is important because it will help you develop a strategy and a plan for your sale.

Setting a timetable

You're going to have to decide how quickly you need to sell your house. Each of the reasons mentioned above for selling your home presents you with a different timetable. This is crucial because you will need to find out how long it takes for houses similar to yours to sell in your market area, and factor that into your plan. Here are some considerations when setting the timetable:

If you plan to move in time to enroll the kids in school in September, does that mean you have to list the house for sale in January? or April?

This will vary in different market areas. In one town, it could take three or four months to sell a property, while in another area, you may expect to sell within a week or two.

The market value of the house is also a consideration in setting the timetable.

In most areas, houses in different price ranges take different lengths of time to sell. For example, a low priced home may sell much more quickly than a very expensive house.

The economic forces of supply and demand are always at work in the housing market.

If there are many houses similar to yours currently for sale, it is likely that your house will take longer to sell. In an area with a significant number of senior citizens, ranch-style homes on one level may be in demand, while homes with a lot of stairs may not sell as quickly.

Research is required and many factors must be considered when establishing a timetable.

Buy first *or* sell first?

This is one of the most difficult parts of your decision-making process. Should you sell the house you're living in and then shop for another house? Or is it better to buy the house you want first and then put your house on the market? Can you do both at the same time? With either course of action you have to consider the positive and negative aspects.

Selling first.

If you decide to sell the house you're living in first, this presents you with stress and uncertainty.

Let's assume you have accepted an offer and set a closing date for the sale of your house. You are now faced with the task of finding another home within a specific time frame. You now have a deadline that is absolute. You MUST find a house and buy it quickly.

What if you have trouble finding the house you want? What if you do find a house you love, but the seller cannot or will not offer you the closing date you need? What if the structural inspector discovers problems that you are not willing to accept?

Buying first

If you decide to buy the house you want first, this presents you with stress and uncertainty. (Sound familiar?)

OK, you've found the ideal house and your offer has been accepted. You now have to get your current house sold, and you need to do it immediately. You may be faced with the closing date approaching quickly, and your house hasn't sold yet.

What if the house doesn't sell? What if you get an offer right away, but the buyer backs out of the deal after three weeks? What if the structural inspector discovers problems that will delay the closing?

You see the dilemma. In both scenarios, you are dealing with uncertainty. Lots of anxiety. Either way, you may be painting yourself into a corner. Here is a list of the pros and cons:

PROS AND CONS:

Selling first

PROS:

You know the house has sold. (Whew)

You can now go house hunting knowing exactly how much money you will have in your pocket from the sale of the first house. The anxiety of wondering how much it will sell for has ended.

There is a certain relief knowing that the burden of the sale is over.

CONS:

You are faced with limited time to find another house.

You may not find the house you want. You could be pressured to buy a house you do not really like, or in an extreme case, be forced to move in with your parents.

Buying first

PROS:

You know you have the house you really want.

CONS:

Your current house may not sell before the new one closes. This could force you to abandon the purchase of your dream home.

This situation could also put you in a legal bind. If you are contractually obligated to buy the new house, you may not be able to withdraw from the transaction. By canceling the sale, you could possibly forfeit your deposit or face a lawsuit. Obtaining bridge financing may or may not be an option for you in this case.

Either one of these scenarios is uncomfortable for a home seller.

My advice on this dilemma is simple: you must weigh the alternatives and decide what is most important to you; which situation are you most comfortable with? Ask yourself these questions:

What is most important to me?

Is it more important to find my dream home, or make sure my house is sold?

Is it more important to be certain that I have secured a buyer for my home before moving forward with a purchase?

I have found through experience that the point of view on this issue is about 50/50; that is to say, about half of sellers feel it's more important to find the right house first. They insist on the security of knowing that they will have a place to live. People for whom the primary motivation is to find a particular house or live in a certain neighborhood will opt to buy first. On the other hand, about half feel it's more important to be sure their house has sold, so they're not 'stuck' with two houses.

For some, the uncertainty of not knowing if and when the house will sell is too great. This could also become a financial burden they cannot bear.

The inventory of homes for sale will also weigh on this decision. Knowing that there is an ample supply of homes for sale in the neighborhood where you want to live may ease your concerns about selling your house first. Conversely, desirable homes in short supply might cause you to consider buying first. You will need to do some market research to obtain all the information possible to make an informed decision.

Market conditions should also be considered in this decision. If you know that homes like yours sell very quickly in your area, then you might feel secure in buying a house first before listing yours for sale. Your Realtor will be able to provide you with valuable information about the current real estate market.

The Synchronous Sale

Many home sellers attempt to make the purchase and sale transactions simultaneously:

A) You put your house on the market, then immediately begin your search for another home. Your search continues as your current house is seen by prospective buyers, and hopefully, your house will sell in the same time frame that you find a new house. You make an offer, and try to coordinate the closing dates of the two properties.

B) You find a house you want to buy, make an offer and then list your house for sale as quickly as possible. If things work as intended, the closings for both houses can be scheduled to coincide.

This simultaneous scenario is an ideal situation, but it is also a balancing act. A concurrent sale will not always work as planned. The primary difficulty with attempting both transactions at the same time is that sometimes your house doesn't sell when you expect it to, or as quickly as you need it to sell.

Before you attempt a synchronous sale, you need to have a plan. The first step to resolving this situation may be to speak to a bank, mortgage broker or loan company. Professionals in the mortgage business commonly have loan programs that can help you. They are familiar with this situation and deal with it on a regular basis. Bridge financing can be arranged, or perhaps a home equity loan to make the home purchase possible.

SELLING
WITHOUT A REALTOR

Selling a house is like
selling a car, right?

Do I really need a Realtor?

This is a question I hear often. Should you try to sell your house without the help of a professional? Some people wouldn't consider trying to sell their house without one, while others imagine selling a house is easy, like selling a used car or a piano. Can you try to do it? Of course the answer is yes. But if you are considering selling on your own, think about this:

87% of sellers who attempt to sell their house 'For Sale by Owner' ultimately list the house with a Realtor.

Why? Simple – *The house did not sell.*

And why not? That's not quite as simple. Frequently the answer is underexposure. Marketing a home has become very sophisticated. The days of a sign on the lawn and an advertisement in the newspaper are long past. That may be a great way to sell a car or lawn mower, but your house is worth at least a thousand times what your lawn mower is worth. Do you actually believe it should be marketed the same way?

GET REAL.

What a Realtor does for you.

The things I've learned in this business have made me realize that I would not attempt to sell a house without the help of a Realtor. The complexity of the transaction, the legalities involved, and the simple fact that it is a very time-consuming, detail-laden process are a real deterrent for most people. Also, the emotional attachment to a house is an impediment for many sellers. A Realtor offers impartiality, which is a necessity for a successful home sale. If that's not enough reason, here are a few more:

Safety.

When you put an advertisement in the paper, anyone can knock on your door and ask to see the house. Even if they call for an appointment, you know nothing about them.

We are living in a time when people put multiple locks on their doors and spend large sums of money on elaborate alarm systems. Anyone who comes in contact with our children has their background investigated. We worry constantly about our own security and that of our families. We hear stories in the news about home invasions resulting in major loss and sometimes death. This may be a rare occurrence, but do you really think allowing a total stranger into your house is a good idea? Someone you know absolutely nothing about? Your family's safety and security are definitely a major concern.

Most buyers use a Realtor to search for a house.

Over half of home shoppers search for a house *only* with a Realtor. If you try to sell on your own, you've instantly lost over half of your potential buyers. Every Realtor has a pool of buyers waiting for the right house to come on the market. At any point in my real estate career, I have had at least two or three buyers, and sometimes as many as eight to ten buyers looking for homes. In a real estate transaction, having more potential buyers viewing your house translates to greater exposure and the possibility of more offers and a higher sale price. *Is it really to your benefit to ignore more than half the potential buyers for your house?*

Financial Qualification.

This is the *number one reason* real estate transactions fall apart: Failure to obtain a mortgage. How do you know if the people looking at your home can afford to buy it? If the buyers have not spoken with a bank or mortgage company, they may not even know how much they can afford to spend.

Realtors screen clients to make sure that they are financially able to buy a house. No Realtor will waste their time or their client's time showing homes to people who are not financially qualified. A Realtor's clients are pre-approved for a mortgage by a professional. Their customers are only shown houses they can afford to buy. This is not possible for you to do.

Financing Alternatives.

It's very rare for someone to buy a house without a mortgage. Not many people have that much cash in the bank. Frequently, buyers don't know what they can afford, or how much the monthly payments will be. Real estate companies provide a wide range of financial options for their clients. It's not uncommon for buyers to realize they can afford more than they thought they could after consulting with a professional about a mortgage.

Enhancing your home.

Realtors are experts at what makes a house sell for more money. They know every device and technique to make your house more appealing to buyers. Home enhancement recommendations are one of the most valuable services a Realtor can provide. Your Realtor will walk through your house and examine it thoroughly, then make suggestions. This information is worth its weight in gold. It's not unusual for someone who follows their Realtor's advice to make minor repairs, replace things, paint here and there, add a few plants, etc., to discover that the house can be listed for sale for an additional $5,000 to $10,000 or more.

Negotiations.

In every home sale transaction there are matters to be negotiated. Having someone represent you who has your interests and is not emotionally involved will save you money. Price, terms and conditions of the contract and inspection issues all must be agreed upon. A veteran Realtor's negotiating skill will prove to be a huge asset throughout the sale process.

Legal Considerations.

There are a myriad of legal details, discrimination laws, disclosure laws, etc. all of which any Realtor deals with on a regular basis. For example, do you know where you stand legally regarding asbestos removal? Radon gas? Oil tank removal? Seller disclosure? Lead paint? Discrimination? A problem with any one of these can really mess up your transaction. Realtors contend with many matters that you probably haven't even thought about. Your Realtor will provide information on the issues involved and can recommend a competent, experienced real estate attorney.

Details, Details.

A major part of the job for a Realtor is managing the trans-action. In any real estate deal, there are hundreds of details that would keep you busy for weeks. I was not surprised at the result of a national survey showing that home sellers felt the most valuable service provided by their Realtor was transaction management – handling of all the details on a day-to-day basis.

Setting the right price.

This is super-critical. And it's not as easy as you think. Your house isn't necessarily worth what you think it is. It could be worth a lot more or much less than the house next door to yours. A Realtor is an expert on your local market and can help you arrive at an asking price that will help you get the maximum dollar amount and result in the quickest sale.

Exposure, Exposure, Exposure.

Everyone knows that the most important consideration when buying real estate is Location, Location, Location. When selling real estate, it is Exposure, Exposure, Expo-sure.

Marketing is what brings buyers to your front door. As a home seller, you want *every* potential buyer to know your house is on the market, and not just in your immediate area. A lot of home buyers come from outside of your area, even from other states.

More Showings=More Offers=Faster Sale

The challenge is to get potential buyers to view your property. Large real estate companies have invested millions of dollars on market research and have developed extensive marketing plans that include many different ways of exposing your house to potential buyers. Most of these are not available to you as a 'For Sale by Owner' or FSBO. Here are a few of them:

The Multiple Listing Service. This is a system of computerized listings of homes for sale that is available only to real estate professionals. The minute your home is listed for sale, thousands of Realtors have access to the information and can pass it on to clients waiting for the right house. Your Realtor can make additions or changes to your listing instantly.

Nationwide relocation networks. Most Realtors are part of a company with large corporate clients who use their company to relocate employees being transferred. This provides a continuous 'pipeline' of buyers to your area.

Regional or national referral networks. Many Realtors belong to networking groups with other real estate professionals, who refer customers to each other all through your area and across the country.

Homebuyer magazines. Many companies use real estate magazines to advertise their listings. These have wide regional distribution and are very popular with buyers.

Websites. Whether you are a computer person or not, you know what kind of marketing clout the Internet has. Large real estate companies have a dominant Web presence. The Internet is the place nearly all home shoppers begin the search for a home. It gives your property instant worldwide exposure.

If your home isn't prominently displayed in national websites, most home buyers will never even know about it.

Newspaper advertisements. This is one phase of marketing you can do yourself, but it's easy to make a costly mistake.

DID YOU KNOW: *Only 5% of homes are sold as the result of a newspaper advertisement?*

Some large real estate companies are abandoning print advertising altogether because it is not cost effective. If you decide to use newspapers to advertise your home it is vital to know:

- *Which paper gets the best results?*
- *When is the best day to advertise?*
- *What size ad should you place?*
- *Where in the paper should it appear?*

Real estate companies have done extensive market research. Your Realtor has a lot of experience in local marketing and knows how to get the best results. Advertising in a newspaper you think your home would look good in may be a complete waste of money.

Quick Story – *Several years ago an agent I know listed the house of a high-powered attorney. The attorney insisted that the best place to advertise his house for sale was a regional law journal. Against the Realtor's advice, he placed the ad himself. The ad generated **NOT ONE RESPONSE**.*
*This was an **$800** mistake!!!*

AND THE NUMBER ONE REASON TO USE A REALTOR:

Houses listed with a Realtor sell for 16% more money!

If you are planning to try to sell your house as a FSBO, **THIS IS THE MOST CRITICAL PIECE OF INFORMATION:**

According to a nationwide study by the National Association of Realtors and published in every major newspaper in the country, homes sold using a real estate professional sold for 16% more than houses sold For Sale by Owner.

COLOSSAL MISTAKE

TRYING TO SELL YOUR HOUSE WITHOUT A REALTOR

The two most important things to a seller are:

1. Getting the best price
2. Selling quickly

When you choose to sell your house For Sale by Owner, you are saying, in effect,

"Those two things aren't important to me".

If you haven't seen the benefit of employing a skilled real estate professional, you're not paying attention.

HIRING A REALTOR

All Realtors are
not created equal

How do I find the right Realtor?

Most Realtors get the bulk of their business by personal referral. Satisfied customers are always the best source of new or repeat business. Ask friends, neighbors or co-workers who sold them their homes and find out if they would recommend their Realtor.

If you can't get a recommendation from friends, you'll have to find a Realtor yourself. Most towns have several large real estate offices. This does not mean that you won't find a good Realtor at a small independent office, but larger companies and national franchises tend to have greater marketing resources, more agents, larger relocation networks, more clients by referral, more comprehensive marketing plans, etc.

Comparison Shop.

The best way to find the right agent for you is to interview and compare Realtors. Call three local real estate offices and ask to speak to an agent. Explain that you are interviewing Realtors to sell your home and schedule an appointment for each one to visit. Usually, the agent will want to walk through your home and make some notes, ask questions, then make an appointment to return and present a comparative market analysis and marketing plan.

The Realtor will return to your house to present the market analysis. This is the result of a couple of hours of research to determine the approximate value of your house. A Realtor is an expert on the current housing market, and he or she will look at every house in your area that is comparable to yours and determine the estimated market value of your home based on this information. Realtors routinely spend several hours each week visiting houses that have been newly listed for sale. This familiarity with the market is a huge benefit to you. It is their way of keeping on top of a constantly changing housing market. They will use their expertise and experience to recommend a list price for your home. A detailed marketing plan will also be presented.

Interviewing a Realtor

An active, experienced Realtor will answer any of your questions and will be able to give you a very good idea of how much you will be able to realize after the sale of your home.

Questions to ask a Realtor

Are you a full-time Realtor?

COLOSSAL MISTAKE

HIRING A PART-TIME REALTOR

NEVER hire a part-time Realtor. You are paying for full service. Why would you want to pay a full commission for part-time service? If the Realtor has another job, don't waste any more of your time or his. Thank him politely and move on. There are too many important details to your transaction, and too many great Realtors.

I have never seen a client properly served by a part-time Realtor.

They do not offer the familiarity with the market that is an absolute necessity to marketing your home correctly. They do not have the requisite availability to handle all of the details that arise. Would you consider flying with a part-time pilot? If you were going through a nasty divorce would you hire an attorney who doesn't handle matrimonial cases full-time? Remember that Realtors are professionals. Hiring your aunt's co-worker's sister who sells real estate on the weekend is a really bad idea.

Why should we hire you?

A veteran Realtor should have a good answer for this. They should be able to show you that they are experienced and competent, and have a thorough knowledge of the local market area. If you're not comfortable with the answers, consider using another Realtor. **Trust is important.** This cannot be over-emphasized. If you don't feel that this person would do the best job selling your house, choose someone else.

What makes your company different?

Every real estate company has an extensive marketing plan. It should include all phases of how your home will be marketed. Signs, open houses, direct mail, Internet exposure, different types of advertising, etc. You should be completely convinced that this company will do a thorough job of exposing your home to prospective buyers.

Tell us about our market area.

The agent should know:
- How many houses have been sold in your town in the past year
- The median selling price in your market area
- Average number of days on the market
- Percentage of change in recent years
- Number of houses on the market right now
- How does the trend look
- What is the competition in your price range

Choose a good listener

Realtors are talkers. Most Realtors are well-informed about real estate, local politics, culture and schools and can chat for hours. Many are anxious to show you how much they know. Some just love to hear themselves talk.

Great Realtors are good listeners. When interviewing Realtors, try to pick one who is a good listener. What questions did she ask you? Did she inquire about why you are selling? Does she understand your needs? Did she really seem to care about your situation?

Select a Realtor who truly listens to your comments and understands your concerns. A Realtor who is thoroughly familiar with your needs is much better prepared to make decisions that are in your best interest throughout the transaction.

Ask for references

Prior performance is the best judge of future performance. Most Realtors will present letters and cards from past customers. A testimonial from a satisfied client is a very powerful tool for anyone in business.

Every real estate agent has a list of past clients. Ask if he is willing to share that list with you. Call several of them and ask for a candid evaluation.

If you recognize an agent's name from a sign on a property for sale, call that seller and ask if the agent is doing a satisfactory job.

COLOSSAL MISTAKE

CHOOSING A REALTOR BASED ON A PRICE OPINION

When selecting a Realtor to market your home, make the selection based on reputation and marketing plan. **NEVER** choose a Realtor based on a price opinion.

Your home has a value. That value is market-driven. That means it is worth what someone will pay for it. The Realtor is only giving you a professional opinion based on his or her knowledge of the market. Don't fall into the trap of selecting the Realtor who gives you the highest price opinion. This is only a professional estimation based on research. It is not absolute. Remember, *you decide the listing price*, not the Realtor. The Realtor presents the market analysis and recommends a listing price. Ultimately, you make the decision.

Your best course of action is to choose the Realtor whose marketing plan you're most satisfied with. Once you have made the selection, consult with the Realtor you've chosen to set the listing price.

Unfortunately, as in any profession, there are a small number of unscrupulous people in the real estate business. The practice of "buying a listing", although unethical, does occur on occasion. The real estate agent will ask what price others have recommended and then suggest an unrealistically high price. *This is an empty promise.* Basic psychology suggests that some sellers will choose that agent, believing they can get more money for the house. When the house hasn't sold weeks later, you'll get a phone call saying, "I guess we priced it too high." By this time, the initial enthusiasm has gone and potential buyers have disappeared. Falling for this tactic will end up costing you money as your house takes longer to sell.

If any agent says, "You can get more money for your house if you list it with me," **YOU ARE BEING TOLD A LIE**. Politely ask that Realtor to leave. Any Realtor making such an outrageous claim should lose their real estate license.

Remember, your home's value is market-driven. Imagine how you would react if a stockbroker said, "You'll get more money for your stock if you sell it through me." This is impossible. A stockbroker has no control over the value of a stock. You would be angry that he tried to make a fool of you. *A Realtor has absolutely no control over the value of a house.*

Discount and Limited Service Brokers

COLOSSAL MISTAKE

LISTING FOR SALE WITH A DISCOUNT BROKER

Never in history has the saying ***"You get what you pay for"*** been truer. Many outrageous claims are being made by discount brokers and limited service Internet companies that are simply false. Some stretch the truth, while others tell outright lies. Many are just trying to get your money.

The distressing fact is that many consumers are drawn in by these companies, lured by the prospect of a low commission. Sadly, I will draw a parallel to the car business: How many times have you seen a car advertised for sale at a price that seems unbelievably low? When you get to the dealer, the car you want is much more expensive. It has been my experience that Internet brokers simply do not deliver what they promise.

There is a discount Internet real estate company operating in my area which I will call Company X. Company X advertises a 3% commission and claims to be a 'full-service' company. However, they have just *one agent* responsible for *five counties* and about *one hundred* homes listed for sale. How can that be full service?

Quick Story – *I showed a house listed by Company X. While my clients were walking around the house, the sellers pulled me aside and asked, "Can you reach our agent? He's not returning our calls." I was astonished. Since that time I have spoken with other sellers who listed with Company X, and they confirmed what this seller had told me. Once the agent had obtained a signed listing, the agent disappeared, offering little help to the homeowners.*

Another Quick Story – *Twice in recent months, a house listed for sale by Company X did not sell during the six month listing period, and the homes were then listed for sale with my company. They sold within two weeks!*

If it sounds as though I don't like this company, you are correct. I welcome legitimate competition. It's dishonesty that I resent. If this company were to say, "We list your house for a 3% commission, but we don't provide the same services that other companies do," I would respect that. Making the claim that they are a full-service company offering a reduced commission is a blatant falsehood. They have left many sellers frustrated and angry.

If you do choose to list your house for sale with a discount/limited service company, do your homework and go into it with your eyes wide open. Be sure you know exactly what you're getting for your service fee.

I've chosen a Realtor, now what?

Once you've decided which Realtor is best for you, the Realtor will present you with a listing contract. This is the document you sign to list your house for sale. Like most business agreements, many points of a listing contract are negotiable.

Most listing contracts are standard forms, but read it over carefully. Ask questions. Always understand what you're signing. Ask under what circumstances you can cancel the contract. Do you have the right to withdraw the house from the market if your job transfer is canceled? What about sudden illness? You never know when your circumstances might change.

Term of the listing.

This is negotiable. In most areas, the typical listing is six months in length. If you live in a "Hot" market area, and your house is in excellent condition, it may sell in several days if priced correctly. If you're in a not-so-hot area or your house is in not-so-great condition, it could take months to sell. Discuss this with your Realtor. A minimum of three months is recommended for the Realtor to properly market your home.

The Commission.

Also called the fee for service, this too, is negotiable. The Realtor will tell you the fee their company charges. It is most often a percentage, commonly 5% to 7%, but it can also be a fixed amount. If you're not satisfied with this, try to negotiate, but remember:

You get what you pay for!

Let's say that you're interviewing three Realtors to market your home. The first two will list your house for a 6% commission. The third offers to take the listing for a 4% commission. Although the prospect of saving money is tempting, this should send up a red flag. How can an agent provide the same service and marketing for substantially less money? What services will be reduced or eliminated for the lower fee? Where will the agent cut expenses? A discount commission should make you suspicious. If this agent tells you he or she can provide the same service for a discounted fee, you want to ask how that's possible. The agent may be telling you what you want to hear just to secure the listing.

*Keep this in mind: if you are negotiating and the Realtor concedes quickly and agrees to reduce the commission without strenuous objection, what does that tell you about his negotiating skills? When you receive an offer for your house, will he fight to obtain top dollar for you? Or will he give in too quickly just to make the deal?

Another important consideration: If most houses for sale in your market area are offered for a 6% commission and your home is offered for a 5% commission, your home may not be shown as much. Think about this - if there are eight or ten similar houses on the market and they all offer a 6% commission except one, which one do you think will be shown last? Which house might be passed over? Most reputable Realtors believe this to be unethical, but anyone who has been in commission sales knows that the product that pays less is usually presented last. Does any salesman show the least expensive model first? A real estate professional should show all homes in a particular price range, but presenting your home for sale at a reduced commission may leave you at a competitive disadvantage.

Conversely, if most homes for sale in your market area are listed for a 6% commission, listing yours for 7% might cause Realtors to take notice and could make it rise to the top of their list, resulting in a faster sale.

Commission Splits

Once you have agreed on the commission, ask the Realtor how that fee will be shared with the buyer's broker. Most reputable companies have a policy of splitting the commission 50/50 with the office that brings the buyer to the table. That means half of the commission will go to the company marketing your house, and half will be paid to the company representing the buyer. If your broker is receiving a 6% commission from you and offering less than half of that (i.e. 2.5%) to the buyer's broker, this is not in your best interest. You should insist that the commission be shared equally with the buyer's broker so you will not be at a competitive disadvantage.

The commission is normally split four ways, between the real estate companies and the agents involved. Sometimes, they're also paying a referral commission to another agent or company, which means the commission is sometimes being split five, or even six ways.

CHOOSING AN ATTORNEY TO REPRESENT YOU

Do I really need an attorney when I sell my house?

CHOOSING AN ATTORNEY

In most states, you will need an attorney to close title on the sale of your house. In states where an attorney is not normally used, a title company will conduct the closing. In the state of New Jersey, where I am a Licensed Real Estate Broker, an attorney is not a legal requirement. You may complete a house sale without an attorney, but I strongly advise my clients against it.

COLOSSAL MISTAKE

NOT USING AN ATTORNEY
FOR YOUR HOME SALE

The price an attorney charges you is a bargain compared to the alternative. The attorney will protect your interests from the beginning of the transaction to the closing. He or she will work closely with the Realtor to help you through the transaction and will endeavor to make it conclude as smoothly as possible. There is also a certain piece of mind knowing that every legal detail is being handled properly.

If you use an attorney for your transaction, the cost is usually a flat rate. If you should decide to handle the transaction without an attorney, remember this: If you run into a problem midway through the transaction and it becomes necessary to involve an attorney, you will be charged an hourly rate. This would be *much* more expensive.

Questions to ask.

What do you charge?

Try to use an attorney who charges a flat rate. Hourly rates can add up very quickly. With a flat rate there are no surprises. Ask your Realtor about the customary range of prices in your town.

What towns do you work in?

You want an attorney from the area where you are selling the house. It is important that your attorney has knowledge and experience in the local real estate market. An attorney who practices out of the area or from another state may lack that crucial familiarity.

Do you specialize in real estate transactions?

COLOSSAL MISTAKE

CHOOSING AN ATTORNEY WHO DOES NOT SPECIALIZE IN REAL ESTATE MATTERS

You want to hire someone who routinely handles real estate transactions. Real estate law is an area of specialization. A divorce attorney who handles a real estate closing every so often might not be the best choice.

Quick Story – *I sold a house to a couple related to a tax attorney. Although he had little experience with real estate transactions, he insisted on handling the deal. His inexperience soon became apparent to me and the seller's Realtor, as he obviously was not familiar with the process. Due in part to his ineptitude, the parties to the sale reached a stalemate over a structural issue. The seller's Realtor and I intervened and quickly helped negotiate an equitable solution to the impasse.*

On the day of the closing, we sat in his office for nearly four hours because he had incorrectly prepared the legal paperwork. It had to be completely re-printed. As we walked to the parking lot after the closing, the other attorney told us he'd never seen such amateur mistakes. It was the longest closing I've ever attended.

SETTING THE ASKING PRICE

My house is much nicer
than my neighbors house.

The best asking price for your house

Determining the best list price for a house can be challenging for the inexperienced. Setting the asking price requires more than just "guesstimating" the value and placing that price on the property. As you look at recent home sales in your town, not all similar homes are comparable to yours. If the sale price of similar homes in your neighborhood has changed over the past six months, does that mean your house should be priced higher or lower than those homes?

These are factors to be considered when formulating an asking price for your house:

Comparable Sales. You will need to calculate where your house should be positioned by evaluating recent sales and similar properties currently on the market.

Your Motivation. As mentioned earlier, your degree of urgency plays a role in pricing.

Property Features. The architectural style of your house, the floor plan and amenities must be taken into account.

Market Conditions. The overall state of the economy must be considered. Current interest rates are a factor, as well as demand for properties in your town.

COLOSSAL MISTAKE

OVERPRICING YOUR HOUSE

Here is a quick news flash for you:

You're not going to find a "sucker" who will overpay for your house.

I've met sellers who actually believed that if they set the asking price at $20,000 or $50,000 above market value that a naïve buyer would appear and pay the asking price.

Today's buyers are much more sophisticated. They have already scoured the Internet and found every house like yours on the market. They may have visited every house for sale in town. They will know at first glimpse that your house is overpriced. Many times, I've spent the afternoon showing homes to buyer clients who walked into a house and immediately noted that it was overpriced.

Savvy buyers will point out that a similarly priced house in the neighborhood has an extra bathroom, was recently painted, or has a larger property, making your house appear less valuable. They will compare your house to others with a very discerning eye, and will quickly reject a house they perceive to be overpriced. *"What are they thinking"* and *"These people are dreaming"* are phrases I often hear.

Houses for sale with too high a price tag will not sell quickly and can become "stale". There's nothing worse than a stale listing. The first question from a buyer is, *"What's wrong with this one?"* They begin to over analyze your home and will frequently decide that if no one wants to buy this house, there has got to be a reason.

Quick Story – *Several years ago I recommended a list price of $299,000 for a house in my town. The sellers insisted that the list price be set at $329,000. "We will reduce it in a couple of weeks if it doesn't sell." Several agents in my office had buyers looking for homes in the $275,000 to $300,000 price range, but they never even saw the house because it was offered for sale above their price range. About four weeks later, after numerous showings but no offers, they reduced it to the $299,000 I had recommended. The house then sat on the market for three months before it sold. They had 'missed the market' by overpricing the house.*

Be particularly careful not to overprice your house in a slower or 'soft' real estate market. Although some sellers have had success overpricing in a robust market, ***I have never seen a client successfully overprice a house in a slow market.***

COLOSSAL MISTAKE

Under pricing your house

This is no better than setting the price too high. You do not want to give the house away. You want a fair value. At least with an underpriced house, it may sell quickly. The only problem - you should have gotten more money. Do not cheat yourself!

Quick Story – *A family friend called me several years ago to tell me she was listing her house with a Realtor who was a lifelong friend but she wanted me to see it before it went on the market the next day. After walking through the house, I asked at what price they would be listing it. The price she quoted, recommended by her Realtor, was about $40,000 less than market value. She informed me that her Realtor was a full-time teacher who sold real estate part-time. (COLOSSAL MISTAKE) The Realtor was clearly not familiar with the current market conditions.*
The next day the house became available and received 12 offers the first day on the market. Realtors and their buyer clients clearly knew that it was underpriced. A bidding war ensued and the house sold for $25,000 above the asking price, still well below market value. The inexperienced seller was delighted.

Two weeks later a smaller house nearby sold for $20,000 more than hers. I don't know if she ever found out about it, but I bet her Realtor didn't tell her.

COLOSSAL MISTAKE

FAILING TO REDUCE
THE PRICE QUICKLY

I have always told my clients "Don't get married to the price." When the house isn't selling, you need to reduce the asking price, and reduce it ***promptly***. This may be one of your biggest hurdles. When sellers set an asking price, they tend to start making financial calculations and decisions with a particular amount in mind. It is an absolute necessity to get past that mindset and reduce the price quickly if you want to get the most money for your house. The first three weeks of the listing are the most important because anyone looking for a house in that price range will have been introduced to the house during that time.

If you do not receive an offer during the first three or four weeks the house is listed for sale, **THE MARKET IS TELLING YOU THE PRICE IS TOO HIGH.** You need to salvage the situation as quickly as possible by reducing the asking price immediately.

Devising a pricing strategy

There is more to setting the asking price for your home than just picking a dollar figure you think would be right. Carefully studying the comparable sales is a good start, but this must accompany a well thought-out plan, a pricing strategy. Be very careful to avoid setting a "dream price" or choosing a price you *want* or *need* to sell your house for. Too many times I have seen this backfire on clients. Having realistic expectations is always the first step to a quick sale.

Determining the best list price should be a hard, cold business judgment, based only on factual data and market trends. It should never be an emotional decision.

Part of your pricing strategy must be planning for price reductions. Simply setting an asking price and saying "I guess we'll reduce the price if it doesn't sell" is a terrible strategy. *This usually results in a listing getting "stale" and the house taking longer to sell and ultimately selling for less money.* You want to set an asking price that will create a sense of urgency and attract multiple buyers.

Create a realistic schedule with specific dates and amounts for price reductions. For example, plan to reduce the asking price $10,000 every three weeks until you receive an offer. This is a good strategy if you want to stay competitive with similar homes for sale.

> # THE AMOUNT YOU *WANT* OR *NEED* FOR YOUR HOUSE IS TOTALLY IRRELEVANT.
>
> # *WANT* AND *NEED* HAVE ABSOLUTELY NO BEARING ON MARKET VALUE

Price groupings

When the decision is made to reduce the asking price, be sure to reduce the price into the next price grouping. Most buyers search for homes in a particular price range, for example $250,000 to $300,000. If your house is listed for $320,000 and you reduce it to $310,000, you are not attracting a new crop of potential buyers. If you reduce to $299,000, a fresh new group of buyers will discover your house. Buyers who could not afford a home over $300,000 will now be introduced to your property.

Quick Story – *I listed the house of a family who insisted on an asking price more than $50,000 above market value. They were adamant about the price, and would not listen to any kind of rationale. I showed them information about every comparable property that had sold in town. There were similar homes currently for sale nearby, all of which were listed for much lower prices. A team of agents from my office walked through the house, and agreement* *was unanimous. It was entirely clear to the impartial eye that their house was worth nowhere near the price they wanted. They were not able to see it objectively.*

They were very slow to reduce the asking price, and the house finally sold about seven months later. The sale price? $60,000 less than their original list price. The house sold for approximately what I had predicted. This house most likely would have sold within several weeks at that price.

How much money was lost during that time? Over six months of paying the mortgage, utilities, maintenance and general expenses - Not to mention the continuing aggravation of daily cleaning, lawn cutting, picking up after the kids and getting the house ready to show…you get the picture. **This was a very expensive mistake!**

Comparing your house to others

It's no longer your home; It's a product for sale.

It must be marketed that way. You must arrive at the asking price and subsequent price reductions with objectivity. This is difficult for many sellers. I have never encountered sellers who thought their house was inferior. *"Our house is much nicer than theirs"* is a phrase every Realtor has heard a thousand times. Guess what?

NO, IT'S NOT.

This is one of the toughest things a Realtor has to tell a client. And we know you don't want to hear it. But you expect nothing less than absolute honesty from your real estate agent.

Read this list carefully:

"Your rooms are small"

"I smelled cigarette smoke when I walked in"

"Your kitchen is older"

"Your yard needs work"

"You have a lot of cleaning to do"

"Anyone can tell you have cats"

If your Realtor is **not** saying these things to you, you've hired the wrong Realtor. These are things you **need** to hear. These are things you *want* to hear. These are exactly the things prospective buyers will be saying.

If there are two identical houses on the market next door to each other, even small deficiencies can make your house worth less than the house next door.

Drama Pricing

Every seller wants a bidding war. A bidding war occurs when two or more buyers make offers for your house. As they bid against each other, this forces the price upward, resulting in a higher sale price. With multiple offers, the final sale price could be substantially above your original asking price.

The best way to create a sense of urgency and trigger a bidding war is "Drama Pricing."

Retailers often use so-called drama pricing to attract customers. An ice cream shop has a grand opening with ten cent ice cream cones. A movie theater has two-for-the-price-of-one admission on slow nights. A start-up airline offers introductory flights for one cent. Low prices always attract bargain-hunters.

Dramatically under pricing your house makes buyers take notice and will very likely cause a "feeding frenzy." This is a guaranteed way to create a sense of urgency and make your home stand out from the competition.

Quick Story – *A home seller in my area recently put a house on the market. Most houses in the immediate vicinity were valued between $1.3 and $1.5 million. The real estate market was slow, so the seller decided to try drama pricing and set the list price at $999,000. Buyers familiar with the neighborhood realized this was a bargain. The* *first day on the market, the seller received 15 offers and sold the house for about 10 percent above the asking price.*

There are potential downsides to drama pricing:

- You are trying to capitalize on the frenzy that occurs in an auction. Bidders might have buyer's remorse the next day if they believe they have overpaid for the property and could withdraw the offer.

- If no offers materialize, it will be difficult to re-introduce the house to the market at a higher price. Buyers already know your bottom line price.

If you decide to try this, set the asking price at your bottom line and wait for offers.

High points – Low points

Be realistic about the value of the amenities of your house. What you consider to be the best elements of your property may be totally undesirable to potential buyers. Below are examples of different opinions people have of some common features:

Swimming Pool
Seller: One of the best features. Used every day of the summer. Center of outdoor family life.

Buyer: Maintenance nightmare. Takes up most of the back yard. Potential safety issues.

Huge Yard

Seller: Loads of room for kids to play and for animals to run.

Buyer: More work needed to maintain yard. Larger property means higher taxes.

Wallpaper

Seller: Love the colors. Matches the furniture and window treatments.

Buyer: Hate the colors. Has to be ripped down. Big job.

Carpeting

Seller: It adds color and texture to the rooms. Feels good under your feet.

Buyer: Cleaning headache. Why would you cover up hardwood floors?

You get the idea. Your personal taste is not necessarily the same as the buyers. Having an unbiased, neutral observer such as your Realtor to advise you can be very valuable.

COLOSSAL MISTAKE

IGNORING YOUR REALTOR'S PRICE OPINION

When your Realtor gives you a price opinion, he or she will substantiate it with factual data about the current market conditions in your town. If you disagree, ask the agent to have other agents from the office walk through your house. Many real estate offices have "Pricing Teams." These are groups of seasoned agents who have proven to be the best at estimating the value of houses. You will get the advantage of many years of experience from a number of experts. They will honestly tell you what they believe your house is worth. Ignoring their advice could be a costly and time-consuming mistake.

Duncan's
Likely Sale Price
Formula

How much can we expect to get for our house?

Most sellers want to be reasonable. They want to get the best value for their homes, and are not seeking to squeeze an outrageous amount of money from the buyers. They sincerely want a negotiation that will satisfy both parties.

The question always comes up, "If we set the asking price for our house at *X* dollars, how much can we expect it to sell for?" Of course, there is no exact answer for this. A knowledgeable Realtor can give you an estimate, but even having a thorough familiarity with your real estate market, it is just an educated guess. No one knows precisely how much your house will sell for.

There is a formula I use as an approximation. This, of course, is not absolute. I am sure it does not apply to all houses in every region, but in my market area, it is *generally* accurate:

The likely selling price of a house drops one percent every 10 days.

That means if you list your house for $500,000, it may sell for full price in the first 10 days. After 10 days on the market, it is not probable that you will receive full price. It is more likely to sell for about $495,000. If the house is still on the market in 20 days, the likely sale price drops to around $490,000. After 30 days, you should reasonably expect to sell for about $485,000. If the house has not sold in 30 days, the price should be reduced if you want to stay competitive.

Here is the likely sale price for different prices and time-frames:

List Price	Days 1-10	Days 11-20	Days 21-30	Over 30	
$200,000	Full Price	$198,000	$196,000	$194,000	R
$400,000	Full Price	$396,000	$392,000	$389,000	E
$600,000	Full Price	$594,000	$588,000	$582,000	D
$800,000	Full Price	$792,000	$784,000	$776,000	U
$1,000,000	Full Price	$990,000	$980,000	$970,000	C E

Although this formula is not absolute, it can be useful if factored into your pricing strategy. It may help you determine what you can realistically expect the house to sell for.

Selling to a builder

This is quick and easy, right?

Selling to a builder

In some parts of the country, there has been a boom in "knockdowns," that is, the knocking down of older homes to build new ones. Most often, smaller, less expensive homes on larger properties are the prime target of investors and builders. They may tear down the house to make room for a new one, or renovate the existing home and resell it for a profit.

This is extremely lucrative for builders when house values continue to increase. In many parts of the northeast, for example, builders are paying $500,000 and up for the privilege of demolishing the house. Within a few short months a new (usually enormous) house appears, priced from $1 million to $5 million, depending on the neighborhood. In the suburbs, these are known as "McMansions" because of their generic similarity and general blandness. This is a highly lucrative endeavor for the investor, with minimal risk. Even in a market slowdown, during which a house may stay on the market for a longer period of time, the builder will still make a decent profit upon the sale of the property.

Builders and investors have mostly relied on Realtors to inform them about knockdown properties. Every Realtor in the business has a few builders they deal with, and any property introduced to the market with knockdown potential creates an immediate frenzy. Within hours of the home appearing in the Multiple Listing System, builders and investors are notified by Realtors.

The potential for large profit has brought many new builders and investors into the marketplace, and they are actively looking for properties to purchase. This has created a relatively new phenomenon in the real estate market: Builders are approaching potential sellers directly to buy their homes. Many have had success going door-to-door in neighborhoods of homes with knockdown and build potential.

One huge advantage of selling to a builder is that no staging of your house is necessary. You will not need to invest any money in improvements or upgrades whatsoever. The builder will purchase the property "as-is". There will be no structural concerns and related problems. You may want to consider a sale to a builder if your house is in poor condition or you can't afford to make needed repairs.

COLOSSAL MISTAKE

SELLING TO A BUILDER
WITHOUT AN APPRAISAL
OR MARKET ANALYSIS

Be absolutely certain that you know the market value of your house before you sell to a builder. He will offer you a price that sounds great and urge you to decide quickly. He may tell you that your neighbors have already sold to him for that price. Don't be too quick to accept the offer.

Quick Story – *A family in my town inherited a house upon the father's death. A builder approached them immediately and offered them $490,000 for the property. He told them that it was a great offer, and the best price they would get for the property in its present condition. They were just about to accept the offer when one of the heirs called a Realtor in my office and asked her for a market analysis. After studying the comparable sales, she believed that the house should be listed for $625,000. The surviving family members agreed to list the house with her. The house received multiple offers immediately and sold for $640,000. Accepting the builder's offer would have been a $150,000 mistake!*

ALWAYS get an appraisal or market analysis first. You may ultimately accept the builder's offer, but at least you made an informed decision.

STAGING YOUR HOUSE FOR SALE

Time to throw away
the half-eaten Twinkies

COLOSSAL MISTAKE

NOT DOING EVERYTHING POSSIBLE TO ENHANCE, IMPROVE, FIX UP, BEAUTIFY, EMBELLISH, AGGRANDIZE AND SPRUCE UP YOUR HOUSE.

Home enhancement is fundamental if you want to get the best price for your house. In the same way that you might spend hours thoroughly washing a car you're planning to sell, your house needs to be prepared for sale in the same fashion. If you really want to get top dollar for your property, a lot of planning and preparation are required.

A Realtor can be a great asset during this process. They know exactly what to do to maximize the value of your home.

You don't get a second chance to make a good first impression.

You have to start by looking at your house objectively, as if you were intending to buy it yourself.

It's no longer your home; It's a product for sale.

Problems that you have overlooked for years or things that didn't matter to you in the past are now essential to a quick, successful home sale. You want your house to look the best it ever has. Everything should *sparkle*.

Exterior

Let's begin with the outside of your home. This is the cover of your book. Buyers approaching the front of the house will form an opinion in the first ten seconds. What will they be looking at?

> **Fence**. A newly painted fence looks inviting and fresh. Peeling, cracked paint looks unkempt and makes it appear that you don't care about your property. If there are any broken or splintered sections, repair or replace them.

> **Sidewalk.** Sweep and remove any weeds. Fix all cracks. If the sidewalk has become discolored, consider a power washing. If sections of the sidewalk have lifted or become uneven due to tree roots or settling, this should be repaired. In addition to looking bad, sidewalk cracks or raised areas are considered to be a safety concern and could become an issue in the structural inspection.

Front Porch and Steps. Older cement tends to deteriorate over time. Any cracked cement or broken bricks should be replaced or re-pointed. The railing must be sturdy and solid. If there is no railing, you may need to install one to meet current building codes.

Landscaping. Manicure the lawn, trim the hedges and patch up any tired spots of grass. Overgrown shrubbery should be removed and replaced. If the front looks really sad, you may want to consider some colorful new plantings to make the area look terrific.

Lights. Are your light fixtures rusty or cracked? Replace them. Make sure bulbs work.

Driveway. If your driveway is dirty, cracked or in disrepair, consider re-sealing it. Remove any weeds. Remove garbage cans from in front of the house.

Paint. One of the least expensive investments with the greatest return is painting. A $15 can of paint could add $1500 to the value of your home. A house that needs painting looks dull and uninviting. If painting is not needed, get out the garden hose and give it a thorough cleaning. Every house needs this.

Siding. If your house has vinyl or aluminum siding, it probably needs cleaning. Give it a good power washing. Stand on your front porch and look closely at the siding. Is it dusty or dirty? Every buyer arriving to view your house will see that dirt.

Roof. If the roof needs repair or replacement, consider this prior to listing the house for sale. If there has ever been a problem with leakage, hire a roofer to examine it and replace any damaged shingles. A roof that is nearing the end of its useful life will probably be an issue when the house has a structural inspection. Replace or repair any damaged leaders, gutters and downspouts. Make sure the chimney is in good repair. Remove old and unused television antennas.

Windows. This sounds like a no-brainer, but you should replace any cracked or broken windows. Paint to freshen up the trim. Wash all windows thoroughly until they *sparkle*.

Front Door. Giving the front door a fresh coat of paint is a great idea. Replace the old house numbers with new ones. New door hardware is a relatively inexpensive way to make the door look new. Make sure the doorbell is in working order. If you have an old mailbox on the front of the house, consider a new, more colorful one. Put out a new welcome mat.

Add Color. Repaint old window shutters or consider putting up new ones. Add window boxes with fresh flowers. Install a festive flag on the porch. Place chairs on the patio or porch with brightly colored cushions.

Creating a mental picture

Get creative by using pictures to make your house more appealing to buyers. If you have photos of your house showing features that may not be visible or obvious because of the season, leave them out for potential buyers to see.

> **In winter** – In many parts of the country, the landscape can look bleak and barren in the winter. Snow may obscure features that are visually attractive in summer. Display pictures of your house with flowers in full bloom and trees flourishing. If you have a swimming pool which is closed and covered in the winter, a summer photo of the pool with warm water glistening in the sun is very appealing.

> **In summer** – What are the features of your home that you enjoy during the winter? Is there a view through bare trees you will not be able to see in the summer? How about a picture of a roaring fire in the fireplace? If selling a ski chalet during the summer, a photo of the snow-covered ground with boots and skis in the doorway might help close the deal.

People make decisions based on feelings.

Buying a house is a sensory experience. That means all of your senses - appearance, odors and sounds. Adding a bird feeder will attract singing birds and give buyers a warm, fuzzy feeling. It helps to create a mood. It can make them feel as if they have returned from their stressful work setting to a more serene retreat.

Interior

It goes without saying that the entire house should be spotlessly clean. If you're not really good at this or you don't particularly like to clean, hire a cleaning crew. If the house isn't immaculate, that's the first thing (and maybe the only thing) the buyer will notice. You should clean your house as though you were going to perform surgery in it.

Priceless Items.

Anything priceless or irreplaceable should be removed from the house prior to listing. Aside from obvious security concerns, items of great value are a huge distraction. You want potential buyers' attention focused on the house, not on the life-sized bronze sculptures or the $50,000 Oriental rug. (Not a big problem for most of us)

Quick Story – *A Realtor from my office listed the house of an art dealer. Throughout the house were fabulous paintings and sculptures, and the agent had to accompany all prospective buyers visiting the property. Numerous remarks were overheard from buyers who didn't think the house would look nearly as nice with their belongings in it. They simply could not picture themselves living there. The collection of expensive artwork was a detriment!*

Clutter.

When preparing a house for sale, clutter is your greatest enemy. It is a major turn-off to home buyers. As we live our lives, we accumulate a lot of personal belongings. You must keep in mind that you're selling the house, not your stuff.

Clutter is not only a distraction, it also makes your rooms appear smaller. You want potential buyers to look at your house as a blank slate, trying to imagine themselves living there. Buyers want to picture where to put their furniture in each room. That is nearly impossible to do with clutter everywhere.

Clutter is not always debris, like stacks of old newspapers or half-full Chinese food containers. It can be valuable property, such as porcelain figurines or antique collectibles. Any items kept in a disorderly way are clutter.

Quick Story – *Several years ago I showed buyers a newly-listed home for sale. The sellers were collectors of beer mugs and fancy beer steins from around the world. They proudly displayed their collection of more than 1,500 in every room of the house. There was even a rack in the bathroom with an assortment from their home country. To the non-collector, it was an unsightly mess. To my buyers it was clearly a deal-breaker. They just wanted to leave. It may have been, in actuality, a nice house, but you couldn't tell with all the clutter. The house took many months to sell.*

When they were first planning to sell, their initial action should have been to package the mugs and put them in storage.

Sometimes, it is difficult to see your own clutter because you have lived with it for years. You may have stepped over something for so long that you just don't notice it anymore. Do you think you may have trouble seeing your own mess? Here is a suggestion: Take a photo of the room and show it to friends. Their reaction will be the same as a buyer's reaction. If they gasp with an expression of horror, you know what you need to do.

Dealing with clutter is simple: GET RID OF IT. You're moving. You have to pack up everything in the house anyway, so now's the time.

Brightness.

A bright house always appears more cheerful and inviting to buyers. If a room is naturally dark or poorly lighted, use lighter curtains and the brightest bulbs possible. Any furniture partially blocking a window should be moved.

Excess Furniture.

This is as bad as clutter. You don't want your rooms to look smaller than they actually are. They will if you have too much furniture, or furniture that's too big for the room. Do you really need two dressers in the bedroom? Would the living room look larger if one of the tables was gone? Would the family room have more open floor space with the sofa against the wall? Does the kitchen have a better flow if the breakfast table is pushed into a corner? Any of these things could make a vast difference in making your rooms look larger.

Photos.

Family pictures fill all of our homes. It's the way we recall our most precious moments in life. We treasure our loved ones and want to remember every event, large and small. This may sound cold, but your personal photos have to go. You want to de-personalize your house when it's for sale. It's very difficult for a buyer to envision living in a house that has portraits of your family everywhere.

It's no longer your home; It's a product for sale.

Don't lose sight of that. You will soon be unpacking your pictures in a wonderful new location.

Quick Story – *I was showing a house to a family with teenage sons. I heard laughter coming from the bedroom and found the boys looking at a framed photo of the husband and wife on vacation at a topless beach. Weeks later, that was the only thing the family remembered about the house.*

De-Personalize.

In addition to photos, any other personal items that could make a buyer uncomfortable should be eliminated. This includes any art objects that might be considered bizarre or lewd. Any item that makes a strong religious or political statement should be packed away.

Odors.

Is there anything more disgusting than foul smells in a house? I can tell you from experience that there is nothing more sickening than walking into a house that smells horrible.

COLOSSAL MISTAKE

NOT GETTING RID
OF FOUL ODORS

Do whatever you have to, but get rid of offensive smells and cooking odors. There is no faster turn-off. The most common offenders are cigarette and pet odors, but many others also qualify as gross.

With any bad odors, there is an immediate perception that the house is dirty. Even if this isn't true, it is hard to overcome the "ick" factor. I have had many buyer clients who simply would not consider buying a house with a tobacco odor. There is a common feeling that cigarette or cigar smoke is indelible; many people believe that you can never totally purge the house of the smell.

The primary culprit of odor retention is fabric. Odors are absorbed by carpet, draperies and furniture. Vacuum and shampoo any carpets or area rugs. In particularly difficult cases, professional cleaning may be necessary. Wash or dry clean draperies. Smokers will probably need to repaint the interior of the house.

If a thorough cleaning doesn't get rid of odors, there are many products on the market that perform well in neutralizing odors, such as Febreze and Air Sponge.

Don't overdo it. You want the house to smell fresh, not like a cheap motel. Be careful not to overuse air fresheners and scented candles. This doesn't smell fresh; it just smells like you are trying to cover something up. Get rid of mothballs - They do not emit a pleasant odor.

Quick Story – *I arrived to show a house a few minutes early. As I waited in front of the home for my buyer clients, I could smell something awful, but I couldn't identify it. We entered the house to the most putrid odor I have ever smelled. It was overwhelming. The homeowners were breeders of show cats and there were more than a dozen cats in the house. My customers insisted on leaving*

immediately, and I told the sellers that they had to do some-
thing about the odor if they truly wanted to sell the house.
They were insulted. I don't think the house ever sold.

Neutralize

This gives potential buyers a better opportunity to picture
themselves living in the house. Older wallpaper should be
removed. Any painting you do around the house, inside or
outside, should be in neutral colors. Consider white or off-
white, and colors like earth tones and pastels. If you do not
want to hire a professional decorator, just ask at the paint
store for advice. Do not forget that lighter colors make a
room look larger.

Room by room

Every room in the house will need attention when you're
planning to sell. Walk through the house with all of your
family members. Take along a large pad to make notes and
assign tasks. Everyone can help to get the house ready for
buyers.

Entry

Create a great first impression. Use fresh-cut flowers or an air freshener. Repaint if needed. Floor

should sparkle. New light fixtures look great. Replace tired light switch plates.

Kitchen

For a lot of people, the kitchen is the most important room in the house. Many buyers will make the decision to purchase right here. Make sure it is immaculate and there are no odors. Put a box of baking soda in the refrigerator. Replace knobs and hardware on drawers and cabinets if needed. De-clutter counters and shelves by removing small appliances, containers and boxes of food. Consider a new floor if needed. Chipped or damaged counters should be repaired or replaced. Straighten and organize cabinets for neatness and additional space. Fresh paint always pays off. Buyers *always* open the oven – it must be spotless. If the oven is greasy, buyers get the impression that the entire kitchen is dirty.

Living Room

Fresh flowers or plants smell nice and look first-rate. Have carpet and area rugs professionally cleaned. Refinish hardwood floors. Add lamps for warmth. Use Pledge or lemon oil on wood furniture. Adding a mirror can make a room look larger and brighter. Clean windows thoroughly. Keep very few items on tables. If you have a fireplace, clean or replace the protective screen as needed. Minimize the number of items on the mantle.

Dining Room

Remove all clutter. Thoroughly clean all furniture including glass in china cabinets. Remove any leaves from the table to increase space. Place four chairs around the table and store extra chairs out of sight.

Bathrooms

Place all cosmetics, etc. in cabinets or drawers. Add an air freshener. Replace shower curtain and towels with bright new ones. Repair cracked and broken porcelain in the bathtub. Re-caulk the tub. Replace the toilet seat. Consider new light fixtures. Clean tile grout meticulously. Make sure faucets do not drip. Flush drains.

Bedrooms

Clean thoroughly. Wash windows. Clean carpets. Use your best bedspreads with pleasing colors. Tables and dresser tops should be neat and tidy.

Closets

Neat and bright closets look larger. If they seem crowded to you, the buyers will feel the same way. Straighten and un-clutter closets; use organizers to increase usable space whenever possible. Consider adding a light. Off-season clothes should be out of sight or in storage.

Stairways

Objects or toys on stairs are dangerous and make the area look disorderly.

Basement

Organize and clean the laundry area. Paint concrete floors a neutral grey color. Check for signs of pest infestation. Clean the furnace and change the filters. Straighten and de-clutter as much as possible. Is the basement musty or damp? Add a dehumidifier if needed. Water seepage will almost certainly be an issue during the home inspection. If this has been a problem, consider waterproofing or installing a sump pump.

Garage

Sweep thoroughly. Clean any stains on the floor and consider painting the floor neutral grey. Reduce clutter by hanging tools and lawn implements on wall racks.

Hiring a professional stager

There are companies and individuals for hire who specialize in staging homes for sale. They normally charge from $100 to $250 per hour to come to your house and advise what is needed to prepare your house for the market.

The service provided by professional stagers can be highly effective. They can range from minor decorating suggestions and re-arranging furniture right up to a major makeover, including replacing all of your furnishings with high-end rental pieces. This may sound somewhat over the top, but just do the math: If spending $5,000 to decorate and rent fabulous furniture increases the value of the house by $10,000, this could really be a wise investment.

COLOSSAL MISTAKE

MAKING EXPENSIVE UPGRADES THAT WON'T INCREASE THE VALUE OF YOUR HOUSE

Spend wisely when staging your house for sale. Avoid expensive improvements whenever possible. The following are maintenance upgrades that are not likely to increase your home's value:

New roof – Buyers can only expect a functional roof that does not leak. If there are leaks, have them repaired. Don't replace the roof unless it is very old or in seriously bad condition. Spending $5,000 to $8,000 for a new roof will not allow you to increase your asking price by that amount.

New windows – If new windows are needed, this is a maintenance issue. It may be considered an improvement, but the dollars you spend will not increase the value of your house by that amount.

New carpet – This is a costly mistake. Today most buyers don't care for carpet; hardwood floors are far more popular. Do you have wood floors underneath your carpet? Remove the carpet and have the floors refinished. No hardwood under the carpets? Have them thoroughly cleaned.

*Quick Story – An agent from my office who specializes in foreclosed properties showed an investor a newly-listed house. She pointed out that the house appeared to be in good condition, with new vinyl siding. Upon entering the house, they discovered the walls **inside** the house had also been covered with vinyl siding. While sharing a hearty laugh, she remarked that it was the only house she had ever seen where you could hose down the dining room. She later found out that the seller worked for a company that installed vinyl siding.*

THE SHOWINGS

Let me give you a tour.

THE SHOWINGS

You've been through this as a buyer, so you have some idea of what to expect. A Realtor will check with your real estate office to make sure your house is still available for sale, and will then call to make an appointment to show it. The agent will give you as much notice as possible when scheduling a showing, but buyers do not always choose the houses they want to see in advance. They may make a last-minute decision at the real estate office, and occasionally there will be a call from a Realtor to visit your house on short notice.

This is my best advice: Bend over backward to let your house be shown. It may not always be entirely convenient for you, but this could be the serious and anxious buyer you have been waiting for.

COLOSSAL MISTAKE

MAKING YOUR HOUSE
DIFFICULT TO SHOW

Be as cooperative as possible. You do not want your house known as a "Problem House". If you only allow showings on Saturday and Sunday afternoons, you are sending the message that you're not really serious about selling your house. Realtors, when forced to conform to restrictive showing times, may avoid showing your house, or worse, forget about it. On numerous occasions I have been forced to bypass a house that my customers might have bought because the house could not be shown.

Of course, there are circumstances when showings must be limited by necessity, such as a newborn baby in the house, or a seller who works at night and sleeps during the day. Overall, it is definitely to your advantage to make the house as accessible as you can.

I recommend allowing your Realtor to use a lockbox to permit access. This makes it possible to show your property when you are not at home. The lockbox is a device which contains a key for your house, and is usually placed on the door knob or front railing. Realtors have an electronic key or a secret combination to open the box and obtain the door key. There are circumstances when the use of a lockbox is not advisable, for example, when there are extremely valuable items in the house, (consider removing these) or if a dog must be removed from the house prior to showings.

Keep this in mind:

Harder to Show = Longer to Sell

Before they arrive

After a Realtor calls to make an appointment, there are a few final things you can do to help make it a pleasing sensory experience for the prospective buyers:

Make it Bright. Open curtains and blinds, turn on lights. A bright house is more appealing and adds warmth. It makes the house feel lived in and friendly.

Music. Subtle background music helps create a mood. Choose classical or soft jazz rather than hard rock or rap music.

Smells. Pleasant smells are welcoming and appreciated. Fresh flowers or potpourri in the foyer are inviting. (Don't overdo it) If you really want to pull out all the stops, the smell of baking bread or an apple pie in the oven is irresistible.

Fire. If the time of year is right, light up the fireplace. This is one of the most powerful ways to create mood. Everyone loves the feel of a warm fire. This also demonstrates that the fireplace is in working order.

Temperature. This may sound like a no-brainer, but make sure the house is comfortable. On a 90-degree day, would you want to walk through a house with the air conditioning off and the windows closed? It is difficult for buyers to appreciate a house when they are in a temperature extreme, hot or cold. Even if the house is vacant, it is to your benefit to maintain a comfortable temperature for showings, any time of year.

During the showing

GO AWAY!

COLOSSAL MISTAKE

FOLLOWING BUYERS
AROUND THE HOUSE

While the house is being shown, you want potential buyers to feel at ease. Some sellers feel the need to follow the prospective buyers around the house, pointing things out or offering a tour. Avoid this unless they specifically request it. It is best if you are out of sight. Let the Realtor show the property. Take the opportunity to walk the dog or step outside to water plants. That way, you're nearby if there are any questions, but not interfering. If you follow buyers through the house, they will feel pressured. They will not comment freely. Most buyers will repeatedly tell you how nice the house is, not wishing to offend. Their remarks may or may not be truthful, and may get your hopes up unnecessarily.

Limiting distractions

Dogs. Most people like dogs, but they are a distraction. Take them for a walk or put them outside. You want the buyers looking at your house, not playing with your pets. There are also people who may be allergic or simply do not like dogs.

Television. Another distraction. Turn it off. Especially if a sporting event is on, the buyers may be more interested in the game than seeing the house.

No Apologies. Don't apologize for the appearance or condition of anything. You might be calling attention to something the buyers would never have noticed.

How you can tell if buyers are serious

The best indicator of genuine interest is the amount of time buyers spend looking at your house. Those with little interest will walk through quickly and leave in a short time. Buyers with more than a casual interest will try to picture themselves living in the house. If they start taking measurements to see if their furniture will fit, they may be seriously interested.

The nature of any questions they ask will also give you a clue to their degree of seriousness. People who have rejected a house will usually not ask detailed questions about the house, the neighborhood and the school system, etc.

While the house is being shown, it is best to let the Realtor ask buyers the appropriate questions. The agent will make every effort to obtain information and gauge their interest.

Be ready with information

Your Realtor has prepared a fact sheet with the significant details about the house. Make sure you have an adequate supply of these. Additionally, keep other information handy in case buyers ask for it, such as:

- Recent utility bills
- Property tax bill
- Property survey
- Floorplan
- List of upgrades you've made
- Warranty documents for appliances
- Condo Association rules or bylaws

PUBLIC OPEN HOUSE

**We're not in the market
for a house,
we just want to see your closets.**

PUBLIC OPEN HOUSE

Open houses are very popular with prospective buyers. As a marketing technique, there are pros and cons. Whether you open your house for public viewing is at your discretion. I have spent many Sunday afternoons at open houses for my clients.

Houses do not usually sell as the result of an open house. Most Realtors stage open houses because their sellers want them to. For the agent, it is an excellent way to meet new customers. If your house is not for them, the agent will show them other properties for sale.

For the protection of your property, I recommend allowing only one couple or family into the house at a time. I lock the door and post an explanatory sign on the door that says something like this:

I am showing this house to another group right now, so please be patient; this house is worth the wait. I will be with you in a few minutes. Thanks.

Pros

- *Newspaper advertisements and signs are a necessity, so anyone reading the paper or driving by will know the house is for sale and may stop in. No appointment is necessary.*

- *Buyers who have not yet established a relationship with a Realtor may visit.*

- *The main reason to hold an open house is this:* ***It just might sell.***

Cons

- *Most of the visitors are not serious about purchasing a house. Open houses tend to attract casual viewers and people looking for something to do on a Sunday afternoon. Half of your neighbors will show up.*

- *Visitors who might be seriously in the market for a house may not be financially qualified to buy your home.*

- *There is always a security concern with an open house. Although incidents are rare, you are opening your door to literally anyone. When your house is shown by Realtors, the buyers have been screened.*

TRY SOMETHING NOVEL

Traditionally, Realtors have staged open houses for the public on Sunday afternoons. I don't know the origin of this practice, but it seems logical considering that in the early days of driving most businesses were closed on Sunday. Morning was for attending Church, and the afternoon became a time to go for a drive, perhaps to visit family, or travel to the mountains or the shore.

I have always been a fan of imaginative marketing. Times are different now and circumstances offer marketing opportunities that did not exist in the past. The entire purpose of an open house is to attract potential buyers to your property. Why not an open house in the morning or evening?

Consider these potential opportunities:

- **Is your house near a train or bus station**? Consider an open house on a weekday from 5-7 PM. As commuters arrive, they may stop by to see your house.

- **Does your town have an evening when businesses are open late?** This is a draw for people who want to shop or have dinner out. Try an open house from 7-9 PM.

- **Is your town planning any special events?** A large number of people attend concerts, parades, rallies and meetings. Plan an open house before or after the event.

- **Do you live near a church or school?** Find out when a large gathering is planned and schedule an open house as the event is ending.

- **Sporting events draw huge crowds.** Stage an open house to coincide with the end of the game.

- **Pick up your local newspaper.** If someone in your neighborhood is having a house sale or garage sale, this could attract a lot of potential buyers.

Here's the bottom line– stage the open house when you have the greatest potential to attract a large number of people. Although most of the visitors may not currently be in the market for a home, they may have a friend or relative interested in moving to the area.

WAITING FOR AN OFFER

Why isn't our house selling?

WAITING FOR AN OFFER

This can be agonizing. If priced and marketed properly, potential buyers are walking through your house regularly. You are trying to be patient, but that isn't easy. People make an appointment to see the house, but then cancel at the last minute. You pick up after the kids and vacuum because potential buyers are coming at four o'clock. They show up an hour late and stay less than five minutes. Others show up early and stay for 45 minutes, leading you to believe they have serious interest. Your Realtor calls back to say they didn't like the house at all. It can be exasperating.

I don't have advice here that will make you feel any better, except to point out that every home seller goes through the same thing.

What to expect from your Realtor

While the house is on the market, your Realtor will be watching every day as the showings proceed. What else is your agent doing?

> **Monitoring the showings** - Watching closely to see how often the house is being shown, and following up by speaking with agents who showed the house for feedback. Sometimes comments made by potential buyers or their Realtor can be helpful.

If the asking price is reduced, your Realtor will inform agents who have shown the property. This may re-kindle interest in buyers who previously rejected your house because of the price.

Continually thinking about your house – A good Realtor will have you in mind every day. He should be frequently reminding other agents about what a great house you have, and how it would be perfect for their customers, etc.

Observing the market – Paying attention to trends in your neighborhood and town. Are homes similar to yours selling while yours is not? Why? Is the market slowing down or picking up? How does this affect your list price?

As your house waits for the right buyer, your agent should update the market analysis every month or so to keep you informed so that you are confident that your list price is in line with similar properties. You should not be at a competitive disadvantage.

Communicating with you – Your agent should be calling you or visiting on a regular basis. He should be discussing the feedback he received from those who have seen the property. An e-mail with information on showings every week is a great idea.

Your Realtor should continue to keep you updated about any new advertising and marketing efforts. You should be made aware of special events, such as an open house day, when all of his company's list-ings in your town will be open to the public on the same day. Events like festivals and parades can draw large numbers of people to your town and are a mar-keting opportunity for your Realtor.

What you can do

Be sure to inform your agent about any changes or improvements around the house. For example: you refin-ished the wood floors; planted new bushes in front; repainted the garage doors, etc. Your agent can add this information to the computerized multiple listing.

Also keep your Realtor informed about any changes that may have an effect on showings of the house. For example, a family wedding is a good reason to suspend showings while the house is full of visiting relatives, or you may want to stop showings during religious holidays.

Why is our house not selling?

This question regularly troubles home sellers anywhere that real estate can be bought and sold.

Everyone wants a quick sale. When the house has been on the market for a long time, the seller becomes anxious and the Realtor is beleaguered.

Fortunately there is an answer to this dilemma.

Here is the solution …

THERE IS ONLY
ONE REASON
A HOUSE DOESN'T SELL

It's all about PRICE.

Stop ignoring the elephant in the room. Sellers don't want to hear it. And they never want to believe it. Sorry, but it is **always** true. If the house is priced correctly, it will sell. This is true of ANY property, from a one-room bungalow to a waterfront mansion on a hundred acres of land. It is true in any market environment, whether it is a booming market or a declining market. All real estate has value.

Real estate markets are highly localized. There is no national real estate market. There are regional and local markets. A booming market in the northeast does not necessarily mean a robust market in Florida. Las Vegas may experience a building boom while housing starts (new construction) in Michigan are down. During market slow-downs, New York City usually remains unaffected, while homes a few miles outside the city may drop in value. In suburban areas, certain counties may experience a decrease in prices while a town just ten miles away has an inventory shortage due to high demand.

Selling in a slower market

Real estate markets are cyclical. What goes down must come up. That has been the story of the real estate market for many years. There are temporary slowdowns, but the market rebounds. Most home buyers are not in the market for a quick turnaround. They are buying a house to live in. Because of this, they are much less likely to be affected by a short term dip in housing prices. I frequently ask my buyer clients if they are on the one-year or five-year plan. If you plan to buy and then sell the property in a year or two, think twice about buying in a declining market. You may not recoup your investment. But most buyers have no intention of selling in the immediate future. They plan to stay five years or longer. Most likely, buyers in this cate-gory will be unaffected by current slower market condi-tions.

Pricing is even more critical in a declining market. When supply exceeds demand, houses have a tendency to take longer to sell. The inventory of homes for sale increases, which means you have greater competition to sell your house. Competition forces prices downward with any product for sale, and this is especially true of real estate.

You may find this helpful if your house has been on the market for more than three or four weeks:

If you've had **many** showings with no offers–
Your house is overpriced!

If you've had **few** showings with no offers –
Your house is BADLY overpriced

You definitely do not want your house in the latter category. If your house is not being shown at all, not only is the market telling you the price is too high, but Realtors are not introducing your house to prospective buyers because of the asking price.

Remember this: *There is nothing a Realtor would rather do than sell your house.*

Realtors live on the sale commission. They love to sell houses. But when Realtors believe the list price is unrealistically high with little chance of selling, they may not even encourage their customers to look at it.

So, consult with your Realtor, take a deep breath and bite the bullet. **Price it right** and your house will sell.

Selling with a lease option

Is there a benefit to selling your house with a lease option? Here's how it works: You offer to rent your house to someone and give them the option to purchase the house at a future date for a predetermined price.

For example, a potential buyer agrees to rent your house for $1500 per month for two years and has the option to purchase the property for $250,000 at the end of the lease. There is typically a payment up front to purchase the option, which is agreed upon by both parties. Sometimes the seller will agree to apply a portion of the rent to the purchase price.

Here are the advantages to the seller:

- You can set a higher selling price than in a normal transaction.
- You can demand a larger monthly rent payment.
- If the renter does not exercise the option to buy at the end of the lease, you keep the money paid to purchase the option.

The lease option is only practical for the seller in limited circumstances. If you need the money from the sale of the house right now, this is the wrong choice for you. The lease option provides an opportunity for the seller if the market is slow or the house has been difficult to sell.

The potential risk for the seller is obvious. With an option to purchase, you are contractually obligated to sell them the house. They have the right of first refusal. If another buyer appears with a much higher offer, you must decline the offer. When the time comes to exercise the option, the sale price could be a bargain for the buyer. If the value of the house has increased, it could be worth more than the buy-out price. If the renter exercises the option to buy the house, the seller will receive less than market value for the property.

If you decide to sell your house using the lease option, an attorney must prepare the contract for your protection.

WE HAVE AN OFFER

Are we done yet?

The offer

The phone rings. Your Realtor is on the other end. She says the four sweetest words you can hear when your house is on the market:

"We have an offer"

You breathe a sigh of relief, but with nervous anticipation. Could this be it? Will we make a deal? Has all the aggravation paid off? What can we expect? Can I finally stop vacuuming every day?

Get Ready

The process of receiving an offer can be handled in different ways. In some cases, your Realtor will present the offer to you over the phone. He or she may want to come to the house to discuss it with you. Frequently, the Realtor for the buyers will want to present the offer to you in person. This is the method I prefer.

Hearing the offer

Many Realtors for the buyer opt for the in-person presentation because they want to have the opportunity to discuss it with you directly and answer any questions you may have about the buyers and their offer. They may want to get a feel for any misgivings you have and address them imme-diately. This is also a much better way for you to familiar-ize yourself with the details. You can ask questions about the buyers: their employment, family members, interests and lifestyle.

Questions to ask

The principal question in your mind is, of course, "How much is the offer?" Don't be so focused on the offering price that you overlook other matters of importance.

Are they financially qualified?

This is of paramount importance. Your Realtor has proba-bly already handled this, but it doesn't hurt to ask. **The primary reason residential real estate transactions fall apart is failure to obtain a mortgage.** If this matter is already settled, it's one less thing for you to worry about. Ask to see a mortgage pre-approval letter from their bank or mortgage company. Know the difference between pre-qualification and pre-approval:

> *Pre-Qualification* – This means someone (maybe not a qualified mortgage rep) has asked them how much money they make and calculated how much they can afford to spend. It is not very incisive, and their credit report is not examined. A pre-qualifica-tion letter is worthless.

Pre-Approval – They have made application and been approved for a mortgage. The mortgage company has checked their credit history and examined their paycheck stubs, employment history and bank statements to make sure they have the necessary funds to make the purchase. With a pre-approval letter in hand, all the buyer needs to do is find a house.

COLOSSAL MISTAKE

DEALING WITH A BUYER
NOT PRE-APPROVED
FOR A MORTGAGE

The pre-approval letter will state the extent of the buyer's financial capability. If they currently own a house, it will specify whether the sale of that house is a condition of the approval. Once they have been pre-approved, the only matter still pending is the appraisal of the house.

Once you have accepted the offer, their bank or mortgage company will send an appraiser to your house. The appraiser calculates the estimated value of the house and forwards that information to the bank or mortgage company. They will then receive final approval which is called the mortgage commitment.

When do they want to close?

This is always an important question and in many cases can be as critical as the price negotiation. The closing date is usually negotiable, but sometimes the seller or the buyer has an inflexible timetable. Occasionally, this can be a deal-killer.

- The house they currently own may be under contract, with a specific closing date that cannot be changed.

- They might have to move in time for their kids to attend school, but it may be impossible for you to vacate that soon.

- They could have a job transfer from another area and must close and move in within 30 or 45 days.

Even if you want to be flexible and make every attempt to accommodate their needs, the problem could be insur-mountable. If you cannot agree on a mutually convenient closing date, you might have to turn down the offer.

Do they have a house to sell?

Most home buyers cannot afford to own two houses at once. If they currently own a house, they usually must sell their house to buy yours. Here are the possible scenarios:

They are moving from an apartment – This is ideal from your standpoint. There is no impediment to their moving at any time. This is a big advantage for you because they are often completely flexible about a closing date, and may even offer to close at *your* convenience. The only possible snag occurs if they are locked into a long lease at their apartment, but they have probably considered this before house hunting.

Their house is under contract – This works well for you in most cases. They already have a tentative closing date for their house, and will work with you to coordinate the closing dates. Insist on seeing their contract of sale for contingencies that may affect your sale. Your Realtor will want to monitor their home sale closely to make sure it is proceeding with no problems.

Their house is currently on the market – You want to ask a lot of questions here. The primary one being, **What if it doesn't sell?** Is the sale of their house essential in order to purchase yours? Have they arranged alternate financing? Could your sale to them be in jeopardy if their house doesn't sell by a certain date?

Their house is not yet for sale – Is it ready to put on the market? Will it sell quickly? Do they need the proceeds from that sale to purchase your home? They should be talking to a bank or mortgage company about bridge financing or other alternate funding.

Selling with a Contingency

Depending on the circumstances, you may want to consider accepting an offer with a contingency to sell. In this scenario, the buyers offer to buy your house with a contingency in the contract to sell their current home. This means that their offer for your house is conditional. You, in effect, have accepted their offer, but given them the opportunity to sell their property while you wait. This is also called the right of first refusal. The contract of sale is not binding until their house sells, and your transaction will not proceed until the buyer's house has sold.

COLOSSAL MISTAKE

ACCEPTING AN OFFER WITH A CONTINGENCY TO SELL

This is never the most desirable offer because of the uncertainty. The buyer's house could take two weeks to sell. It could take two years to sell. Most attorneys will advise against accepting a contingent offer except under very limited circumstances. Attorneys hate ambiguity, and this type of offer is completely open-ended. It has no definite conclusion, and could leave the seller hanging indefinitely. I cannot recommend accepting a contingent offer.

If you do decide to accept an offer with a right of first refusal, consider imposing these conditions:

- Leave your house on the market.
- Continue to allow showings and listen to any offers.
- If another, better offer is received, inform the first buyers that they must drop the contingency or you will cancel the sale.

If the buyer is unwilling to drop the contingency, accept the second offer and cancel the contract you had with the first buyer. Do not jeopardize a good offer by sticking with an uncertain one.

If you are considering accepting a contingent offer, having an attorney review the contract is an absolute necessity.

The offering price

Getting the best price is what the sale process is all about. You have planned for this moment, agonized over setting the asking price, wondered how much the offer will be, and now you are ready. What can you expect?

Above asking price – This, naturally, is the ultimate result that all sellers wish for. It typically happens only in a multiple-bid scenario, when two or more buyers have decided that they must have your house.

Full Price – This is also an ideal situation. You got your asking price. This is common when the house sells quickly. During the first week or two of the listing period, owners expect the house to sell at or near full price. It does not always happen, but it is nice when it does. The likelihood of receiving full price diminishes with increased days on the market. For a home that has been on the market for an extended period of time, it is not realistic to expect a full price offer.

A Reasonable Offer – The term "reasonable" lends itself to be defined by the user, and this also varies in different market areas with different types of properties. In my area, where homes typically sell for an average of 95% to 98% of list price, an offer at 90% of list price may be considered unreasonably low. Generally speaking, an offer above 90 percent of the list price is regarded as reasonable. Your local multiple listing system has information on how much houses sell for, and at what percentage of the listing price.

A Low-Ball Offer – It's not unusual for someone to make an unreasonably low offer. Sometimes buyers feel they can get a bargain if the circumstances are right. For example, an offer $100,000 below asking price is a low-ball offer. Try not to act shocked if this happens.

Offers with Conditions – Buyers sometimes want to make an offer with conditions. For example, they might say, "We will pay you full price if you include the refrigerator", or "We agree to your price if you replace the roof." One common request is for the seller to pay all or part of the closing costs. These are typical requests you may have to consider in the negotiation.

THE NEGOTIATION

You will undoubtedly have an acceptable dollar figure in mind when you list the house for sale. Whether you share this "bottom line" amount with your Realtor is your decision. You may end up getting more or less than that amount.

All home sellers want an offer on their house to be reasonable, although everyone has their own definition of reasonable. Most offers will probably be in the range of what you'll consider realistic and sensible. Real estate agents counsel buyers to make a practical offer that has some possibility of acceptance, perhaps with a small additional increase. No seller responds well to a low-ball offer. Making such an offer frequently taints the process, that is, the sellers immediately become resentful toward the buyers. This does not work in the buyer's favor. Buyers who offer a low-ball amount are *less* likely to get the deal they wanted.

Most buyers don't expect you to accept their first offer. The way the negotiation process has evolved, the first offer is rarely accepted. The buyers have usually calculated a certain amount of flexibility into the offer as you have built that flexibility into your asking price. They chose their offering price expecting that you will make a counter-offer somewhere in between.

When you listen to an offer in person, you will sit with your Realtor and the buyer's Realtor and he will go over the contract with you and answer questions you have posed about the buyers and their offer. When he has finished, he will step out of the room while you consider the offer and discuss it with your family and your Realtor.

Your options:

Accepting the offer – If the offer is for the asking price or above, you will probably accept it. If the price and closing date are satisfactory, this is ideal.

Accepting the offer with conditions - You can make the acceptance conditional. For instance, you may say, "We will accept the offer if you agree to close in 30 days" or "We accept your offer but will not repair the barn."

Presenting a Counter Offer – This is the most common response to an offer. The amount of the offer is less than you are willing to accept, so you give the buyers a price lower than your original list price for them to consider. This counter offer is then pondered by the buyers who may accept it or give you another counter offer. This continues until you have a reached a mutually acceptable price and terms, a "meeting of the minds."

Rejection – This is rarely done, and I don't recommend it. It is more productive to furnish a counter offer, even if it's close to your original list price. It is always better to "keep the ball in the air", rather than summarily dismissing the offer. If you are annoyed at what you consider to be a ridiculously low offer, you do have the option of just saying no.

Your Realtor will prove to be very valuable during the negotiation. He or she has done this many times and is thoroughly familiar with the process. They frequently have a good idea about what people will accept or reject. They also have a good working knowledge of what your house is worth, and they don't want to see you lose a quality buyer. I recommend you listen to their advice.

Your first offer is your best offer.

This is a very well known saying in real estate. It proves to be true more often than not. Far too often sellers reject the first offer, believing that it is too low, or assuming the next offer will be higher. Four months later, when the house has not sold, and the price has been reduced far below that first offer, the sellers are regretful and often bitter.

This does not mean you should always jump on the first offer and accept it immediately, but you should take it very seriously, and consider it carefully even if it seems a little low. Remember: *"A bird in the hand…"* you know the rest.

Quick Story – *An agent from my office showed a house to buyers the day it was listed for sale at $649,000. The buyers loved the house and immediately made an offer of $639,000. The sellers, believing they would receive multiple offers, announced they would wait several days before making a decision. The buyers were annoyed, and continued to look at other properties. They found another house right away, and made an offer that was accepted. No other*

offers materialized on the first house, and several months later it finally sold for $592,000.
This was a $47,000 mistake!

The first offer you receive may not always come together immediately, but that first buyer is usually the one who buys the house. Negotiations can last for a few minutes or for weeks. The buyer may look at other houses and decide that yours is the better value and return to accept your offer.

Multiple offers

When more than one person wants to buy your house, the result is a competitive bidding situation. Although this seems like the ideal scenario from a seller's standpoint, this is a matter that must be handled delicately. If you allow buyers to continue to bid against each other, this can work against you. You do not want to create an auction where the final sale price soars far above the actual value of the property. In many cases, the buyers get caught up in the excitement of the moment and overbid only to have buyer's remorse and withdraw the offer the next day. Every Realtor has been involved in a transaction like this.

The best way to handle this is to ask for a final, sealed bid from each potential buyer. Make it clear to all bidders that you will not entertain a higher offer tomorrow – this is their last opportunity. You can then review the offers and accept the best one.

In a multiple offer scenario, here is what's usually happening behind the scenes: Your Realtor has notified the other Realtors that there are multiple offers. Each bidder is informed of this and has consulted with their Realtor about their offer. Their Realtor has no idea what the other offers will be, and advises the client to make the maximum offer they are comfortable with.

The *kick yourself* Price

In a multiple bid scenario, I advise my buyer clients to consider the *Kick Yourself* price. That is, consider the maximum price the house could sell for that you would be sorry you hadn't bought it at that price. Let's say the house is listed for $350,000 and you offer $355,000. The house then sells to another bidder for $357,000. Would you **Kick Yourself** for not bidding higher? On the other hand, would you NOT **Kick Yourself** if it sold for $380,000?

Using this technique helps buyers arrive at the maximum offering price that they are comfortable with, and will not regret the next day.

Quick Story – *I was the agent for the buyer in a multiple bid scenario. Knowing there were two other offers, I advised the buyers to bid well above the asking price of $699,000 if they wanted the house badly. After prolonged discussion, they would only offer $703,000. They lost the bidding war to another buyer. Later, when they found out the house had sold for $705,000, they were upset - **kicking*** *themselves - for not bidding higher. They told me they would have gladly paid $710,000 for the house. If they had offered that initially, they would be living there now.*

The **Kick Yourself** price also applies to sellers. During the negotiation as you consider the buyer's offer, stop and ask yourself this: If the house is still on the market in three weeks and has not sold, will you **Kick Yourself** for not accepting this offer? Many sellers have looked back in retrospect and regretted not accepting a good offer.

Meeting of the Minds

You have reached an agreement. The points in dispute have been settled. Your house is now under contract. Your Realtor will take the house off the market so you won't be bothered with calls and showings. You don't have to mow the lawn, vacuum the house or pick up after the kids every day. What's next?

THE HOME INSPECTION

Every house has issues. Period.

The Home Inspection

After you have accepted an offer for your home, the buyer will schedule a home inspection, usually within a week or ten days. The home inspection will customarily include:

- Structural Inspection
- Termite/Pest Inspection
- Radon Test

The buyers may also arrange the following:

- Lead-based Paint Inspection
- Well Test
- Septic System Inspection
- Pool Inspection
- Mold Inspection

A structural inspector will spend several hours examining your house for any potential problems. He will be looking for flaws, defects, damage, maintenance problems and anything that might need repair, as well as compliance with current building codes. I highly recommended that you be home for this inspection, to be available to answer questions about the property and your care and maintenance.

If the home inspector finds potential problems beyond his expertise, he may recommend a specialist for an expert opinion.

COLOSSAL MISTAKE

CONCEALING MATERIAL
DEFECTS OF THE HOUSE

Any defect or problem which could affect the value of the house must be disclosed to the buyers. Attempting to conceal something is never to your advantage. The structural inspection will most likely reveal the problem, which then must be rectified, and could possibly scare the buyers away. It can also become more expensive when attorneys become involved and demand multiple estimates for the repair. If you have knowledge of a structural defect and fail to disclose it, and it is discovered after the closing, you will probably be facing a lawsuit.

If you know of something that is wrong with the house, address the problem BEFORE putting the house on the market.

Most real estate companies now use Seller Disclosure statements. This document is completed by the sellers and presented to the buyers. It is a comprehensive questionnaire in which the sellers reveal information about the house. You should complete this form with absolute candor, and to the best of your knowledge. Don't be intimidated by this. The seller disclosure is simply what you know about the house.

Home inspections normally cover the following areas:

Structure
Including structural integrity, walls, ceilings, siding, windows, doors, porches, decks, patios, stairways, sidewalks, garage and driveway.

Foundation
Including floors, framing, load-bearing beams, basement and water penetration.

Electric Service
Including system type and capacity, wiring, panels, fixtures, switches and receptacles.

HVAC
Including heating system, air conditioning, venting, ductwork and proper temperature.

Plumbing
Including hot water heater, water pressure, waste system, toilets, sinks, fixtures, drains and valves.

Kitchen

Including built-in appliances, ranges, oven, cook tops and dishwasher.

Roof

Including skylights, chimneys, gutters and downspouts.

Extras

Including pool, sprinkler system, well and septic system.

Termites and other pests

One problem that occurs with great regularity is the appearance of termites and other wood-destroying pests. Termites, carpenter ants and carpenter bees are very common. In my market area, over 85% of homes exhibit some evidence of infestation or damage caused by pests. In many cases, the homeowner is oblivious to the situation until it is brought to light by the structural inspection.

This is a situation where the buyer will certainly demand remediation. In cases where there are pests but no damage is present, an exterminator is called to eliminate the pests. This is usually not terribly expensive unless the infestation is widespread. However, damage caused by pests can range from negligible to extensive. A house I listed several years ago required over $40,000 in structural repairs due to termite damage.

The structural report

The structural inspector's report will be sent to the buyer within several days. It is comprehensive and includes many care and maintenance suggestions for the new owners. The section of most interest to the seller is the list of items needing repair. These are items the inspector feels require urgent attention before the new owners take possession of the house. The buyers will review the results and respond with a list of items they want repaired or replaced.

Your Realtor will be a valuable asset during this process. His or her job is to help you settle inspection issues and to minimize the cost of repairs to you. The agent for the buyer will be attempting to maximize the gain for their clients. Negotiation is necessary and generally productive in settling structural matters

Responding to the structural report

You will review the list of demands from the buyer and make a decision about how to respond to each item on the list:

Agree to make the repair. I recommend making minor repairs yourself if you have the expertise. For more technical repairs, get several estimates and hire someone to make the required repair. Make sure this can be accomplished prior to closing. Always get proper permits (if required) from the town or county prior to making any repair.

Refuse to make the repair. Tell the buyers that you don't believe it is necessary, or you don't feel obligated to make the repair.

Offer the buyers a credit at closing. At the closing, the amount of money to make the repair will be deducted from the purchase price, and the buyers will have the work done after they take possession of the house.

Negotiate. Offer the buyers a portion of the amount they are requesting to make a particular repair. A common example would be a roof that will need replacement soon. If the estimate for a new roof is $5,000, offer them $2,000. If they decline, increase the offer to $2,500, etc. You will save money.

COLOSSAL MISTAKE

NOT DOING EVERYTHING POSSIBLE TO SETTLE STRUCTURAL DISPUTES

Sometimes, the structural inspection reveals problems that the buyer is unwilling to accept and the seller refuses to correct. At this point, the buyer may decline to proceed with the sale. Responding to this is critical, because being stubborn will definitely not be to your benefit. If you reach an impasse remember this:

If the buyer 'balks and walks' you will have to go through this entire process again.

You will have to put the house back on the market and return to square one. The sale of your house could take months longer, and *the next structural inspection will most likely reveal the same problems.* Any structural issue that arises must be resolved eventually. Is it better to settle it now and proceed to the closing? Or do you want to start all over and wait for the house to sell again?

You do not want to lose a good deal over structural issues.

COLOSSAL MISTAKE

MAKING REPAIRS INSTEAD OF OFFERING A CREDIT

Whenever possible, offer a credit at closing instead of arranging the repair yourself. The rationale is simple: it could end up costing you far more money. When a repair of any kind is underway, the contractor doing the work may uncover additional problems, which then become your responsibility to fix. This could be a costly mistake, and has the potential to delay the closing. Additionally, municipal involvement may be necessary depending on the extent of the repairs. Permits may be needed, and municipal inspections could be required.

Although the preferred method, offering a credit in lieu of making repairs is not always possible. Some repairs may be required prior to closing by the mortgage lender or the homeowner's insurance company. From the seller's standpoint, offering a credit is prudent whenever practical.

One Great Idea

This book is filled with colossal mistakes I hope to help you steer clear of. Here is a great idea that may help you avoid a whole bunch of colossal mistakes:

ARRANGE FOR A STRUCTURAL INSPECTION BEFORE YOU PUT YOUR HOUSE ON THE MARKET

Not many sellers do this, but having a pre-inspection could help you avert a multitude of problems. Ask your attorney or Realtor to recommend a structural inspector. Have a full home inspection done when you first begin planning to sell your house. Be sure to have your well water tested and include a termite/pest inspection and radon test.

The best reason for a pre-inspection is that you now have full knowledge of what's wrong with your house before you begin the sale process. If repairs are necessary, you have control over the choice of contractors and you may also have some control over costs associated with the repairs.

A pre-inspection can also be used as a sales incentive. Prospective buyers are told that a home inspection has already been done and any necessary repairs have been completed. This may serve to ease the mind of a nervous buyer. Offer to let them see the inspection report and repair invoices. The buyer still has the option of arranging their own inspection if they choose to.

Home Warranties

A Home Warranty is a service contract to protect against unexpected repairs. It is available through most real estate companies, and may be purchased by the seller or the buyer. The cost is usually $400 to $600 which can be deducted from the proceeds at the closing. The common term of the coverage is one year. Some companies offer a warranty that begins when the property is listed for sale, with the coverage continuing for one year after the closing. Items covered by the warranty must be in working order, as pre-existing conditions are normally excluded.

Home Warranties have a deductible, usually $35 or $50, payable to the contractor. The remaining balance of the repair is paid by the warranty company.

What is typically covered?

> Electrical System
> Plumbing
> Water Heater
> Furnace/Heating/Duct System
> Oven/Range/Cook top
> Dishwasher
> Garbage Disposal
> Trash Compactor
> Ceiling Fans
> Built-in Items

Optional Items

These items can usually be covered for an additional charge:

Well Pumps
Septic System
Washer/Dryer
Air Conditioning System
Swimming Pool/Spa
Roof

The greatest benefit of a home warranty for the seller is the peace of mind it provides for the buyer. An older house with original electrical service or an ancient furnace could make a buyer nervous about proceeding with the sale. With uncertainty about structural issues a potential buyer will be reassured if a home warranty is in effect.

It could also protect you from a lawsuit if, for example, the furnace stops working the day after the closing. Instead of calling an attorney, the buyer will just call the warranty company, and you've avoided a monumental headache.

Home Warranties are well worth the cost, and I highly recommend purchasing one.

Environmental Hazards

Pass the Aspirin.

ENVIRONMENTAL HAZARDS

Some conditions that may be detected during a home inspection are more serious and could require immediate attention due to their potential to affect the environment. These issues usually must be addressed prior to closing, so educating yourself is a prudent thing to do as a home seller.

These problems may be handled differently in different regions of the country. Be sure to check with your Realtor for information about your legal obligations and liabilities in your state. Your Realtor will know if an attorney must get involved.

COLOSSAL MISTAKE

NOT ADDRESSING ENVIRONMENTAL CONCERNS BEFORE LISTING THE HOUSE FOR SALE

If you are aware of any of these conditions in your home, arrange to have the situation remediated **before** you put your house on the market. Once these matters are revealed in the structural inspection, the buyers, their Realtor and their attorney will want to be involved in every step of the process. They can insist on being informed of any remedial action and may want to be present to observe as work is done. Their attorney could demand the right to select the contractor for the project. Having remediation done before listing the house for sale might save you a lot of time, money and aggravation.

Underground Oil Tanks

Underground Oil Tanks can be a major problem. For many years oil tanks for home heating oil were buried on the property. This practice has been largely abandoned, using instead a tank in the basement of the house. The primary reason for this is the potential for rusting and leakage. Older tanks may deteriorate over a long period of time and develop cracks or holes. This is usually undetectable to the homeowner until a soil test is done which shows leakage. Even small amounts of oil can foul the environment, possibly affecting your water supply. In extreme cases, entire suburban neighborhoods have been contaminated, and rendered water undrinkable.

If your home is currently heated by oil from an underground tank, the best course of action is to buy oil tank insurance **before putting the house on the market**. You may already be insured by your oil supply company, but you definitely want to confirm this.

Some homes currently heated by natural gas may have been converted from oil to gas heat at some point. This is especially common in older homes. This is a question home buyers are sure to ask, and you should know the answer:

Is there an abandoned oil tank on your property?

If the answer is yes, you will need to prove that it was legally abandoned. In many jurisdictions there are legal requirements requiring that the town issue a permit and perform an inspection. In some areas, pumping the tank dry and filling it with sand is acceptable, while in other regions, removal of the tank is compulsory. Check with your Realtor or attorney.

If the answer is no, and you're sure there is no underground tank, the buyers may still want to perform an inspection which involves sweeping the yard with a metal detector or performing a soil test. This is entirely reasonable. If you were buying the house you could insist on it also. In many areas, buyers are demanding that underground tanks be removed. Although this is not inexpensive, it is one way to be certain that there is no contamination.

Cleanup of oil contamination can be a monumental problem. Although this story does not involve an in-ground tank, it presents an extreme case and the result:

Quick Story – *Several years ago, a house not far from mine was receiving a heating oil delivery. The tank, located in the basement of the house, was accidentally overfilled. (I don't know whether it was human error or equipment failure) The oil flooded the basement and seeped through the basement walls and permeated the soil, creating an environmental mess. The owners had to vacate the house for*

*safety reasons and the state environmental authorities got
involved. The house had to be demolished and the contaminated soil completely excavated. The homeowners had
to find another place to live and the situation became an
insurance nightmare that took years to settle.*

Asbestos

For a long time, asbestos was used for its fire-resistant
properties. Many years after its usage began, it was discovered to be carcinogenic. If inhaled, the fibrous material lodges in the lungs, and remains in the lung tissue.
Lengthy exposure may lead to cancer.

Prior to being restricted in the 1970s, asbestos was commonly used in roofing shingles, insulation, siding, ceiling
tiles, etc. Asbestos does not usually present a health risk
unless it is deteriorating. The greatest hazard arises when
it is being removed. During the removal process, dangerous fibers are released into the air where they can be
inhaled.

If asbestos is discovered during a home inspection, the
buyer will demand remediation. This is usually accomplished in one of two ways: removal or encapsulation.

Asbestos Removal

COLOSSAL MISTAKE

ATTEMPTING TO REMOVE
ASBESTOS YOURSELF

This is NOT something you do yourself. It is extremely hazardous. Older homes frequently have asbestos insulation wrapped around basement pipes. It may be very tempting to just pull it down and throw it in the garbage. Don't be foolish enough to try this. Remember asbestos is the most dangerous when disturbed. The particles become airborne and can be inhaled.

If you need the asbestos removed, call a certified remediation expert. You'll appreciate how dangerous the removal process is when you see the extent of the safety precautions. They arrive at your house and drape the affected area with plastic sheeting to prevent asbestos particles from dispersal. Hazmat suits are worn as they carefully remove the asbestos and haul it away in sealed containers. After ventilating the area thoroughly, they conduct an air quality test with electronic measuring devices. No one will be allowed back into the house until an acceptably low reading is attained. This is the only safe way to complete the task.

Asbestos Encapsulation

The other alternative for dealing with asbestos on pipes is encapsulation. This process involves over-wrapping the asbestos while leaving it on the pipes. This has the added benefit of increased insulation, and may be less expensive than removal. Consult with a certified specialist.

Lead Paint

Lead poses a health risk, even in small concentrations. The primary threat in the home is in the form of lead-based paint. Lead paint was used on most homes built before 1940, and continued to be used in many homes built between 1940 and 1970. The use of lead-based paint was banned by the federal government in 1978.

Flaking lead-based paint can be ingested or inhaled and will then accumulate in tissues and organs. Damage to the central nervous system can result from high accumulations. Lead poses an even greater danger to children because of their lower body weight.

The greatest danger occurs when old paint is being removed by sanding. A fine lead dust will become air-borne and permeate the area being sanded. If you decide to do this yourself, be sure to wear the proper protective equipment when sanding. Make sure the room being sanded is well ventilated, and allow sufficient time after finishing for the lead dust to dissipate. **Be absolutely certain that children and infants are not in the house during this process.**

Sellers of homes built before 1978 must furnish information about the presence of lead-based paint to prospective buyers. Buyers must also be allowed the opportunity to perform a lead-based paint inspection. Your Realtor will provide the required forms, and the buyers will be given the pamphlet "Protect Your Family from Lead in Your Home" as required by the federal government.

Radon

Radon is a colorless, odorless gas occurring naturally in soil. It is a by-product of decaying uranium. Radon enters your home through small openings, such as tiny cracks in the foundation. Breathing radon increases your chances of developing lung cancer. It can also seep into ground water, putting homes using well water at risk. Radon exists in every state, but is more prevalent in certain areas. Most buyers will insist on a test to determine if radon is present.

Remediation for radon is relatively inexpensive. Even at high levels, it can be successfully lowered with ventilation equipment. A radon remediation company can be found in any local phone directory or through your Realtor.

Mold and Mildew

There are at least 1,000 species of mold commonly found in the U.S. Only a small percentage of these are associated with health-related problems. Everyone is exposed to many types of mold every day, both indoors and outdoors. Most people suffer no ill effects, but some people are more sensitive and may suffer cold-like symptoms. In rare cases mold spores can cause serious illness.

There is no practical way to eliminate mold. The best way to control it is by controlling moisture. Areas of your house that are chronically damp are susceptible and should be kept dry.

If a home inspector discovers (or suspects) mold, he will recommend mold abatement. This must be carried out by a certified mold abatement company.

Government Inspections

These are entirely separate from the buyer's structural inspection. The county or town where you reside has legal requirements for a property that is changing owners. Every state has building codes and your county or municipality has ordinances which must be observed when a house is sold. This is a matter your Realtor is entirely familiar with, and will help you prepare for the inspections. In some areas, a fire department inspection is necessary for smoke and carbon monoxide detectors, while in other areas, a full certificate of occupancy inspection is mandatory. There are usually charges for these inspections.

Selling a
Vacant House

SELLING A VACANT HOUSE

There are many reasons why you might put a house on the market while it is vacant. You may have had to move out of the area quickly due to a job transfer. Perhaps your grandmother passed away and it is an estate sale. Maybe it was an investment or rental property that you did not live in. Whatever the reason, there are special considerations when trying to sell a vacant house.

Maintenance

In your absence, the house should be kept in the best condition possible, just as if you were continuing to live there.

- **Maintain the yard**. Arrange to have someone cut the grass and keep the property looking nice. Water the plants, bushes and lawn as needed.

- **Remove snow**. In many regions of the country, there is the potential for snowfall. The sidewalks and entrances must be kept clear for buyers to get into the house.

- **Comfortable Temperature**. Keep the house in a normal temperature range, usually 68-72 degrees. It is difficult for buyers to feel at home in a house that's sweltering hot or bitter cold. This is a distraction and a turn-off for most buyers. If your house is heated with oil or bottled gas, make sure there is a sufficient supply to last.

- **Winterize the house**. During cold months, it is best to winterize the house. This is usually done by a plumber who will turn off the main water source and flush the pipes to empty them. This is done to ensure that the pipes don't freeze and rupture.

Security

Hopefully, this is not a major problem in your town. It is still wise, however, to take a few precautions. Whenever possible, it is best to make the house appear to be occupied.

- **Tell your Neighbors**. Let your neighbors know that the house will be vacant and ask them to watch for unusual or suspicious activity. Be sure they have your contact numbers to reach you in an emergency.

- **Timed Lights.** Put several lights on timers. I recommend one in the bathroom. If a burglar is watching the house and sees a light in the bathroom, he may assume someone is home. In particularly crime-prone neighborhoods, consider putting a radio on a timer. Most people believe someone is home if they hear sound coming from a house. If a friend or neighbor is checking the house regularly, have them turn different lights on and off.

- **Newspaper and Mail Delivery.** Be sure to have the mail forwarded or picked up by a friend or neighbor. Stop newspaper deliveries. Nothing screams "WE'RE NOT HOME" louder than mail or newspapers accumulating.

- **Notify your Local Police.** Many police departments keep a log of the homes of people who are on vacation or away on business, etc. If anything should happen, they will have contact information to reach you.

Use and Occupancy Agreements

If your house is vacant and has sold but not yet closed, sometimes there may be circumstances in which the buyer will ask to move into the house before the closing. This might occur for a variety of reasons, but most often happens when the buyer has to close on his house before your closing can take place.

Allowing the buyer to move into the house prior to the closing is not recommended. Most attorneys will deny this request without hesitation, because of the potential problems that can result:

> *Once the buyers have moved in, what if they discover problems that they expect you to fix?*

> *You still own the house. What if a fire occurs?*

Does the buyer pay rent until the closing?

Who is responsible for the homeowner's insurance?

*If something happens causing the sale to be can-
celed, you are stuck with someone living in your
house. Will they leave immediately without being
unreasonable?*

If you decide to let the buyer move in prior to the closing,
your attorney will prepare a Use and Occupancy Agreement. This agreement will address all of the issues mentioned. Your attorney will include language in the
agreement to protect you from any situation that may
arise.

WAITING TO CLOSE

WAITING TO CLOSE

Planning your move

As soon as you have a tentative closing date, you'll want to contact a moving company to make arrangements. Do this earlier rather than later, as movers frequently have full schedules, and it may be difficult to get the date you need. The end of the month is normally the busiest time for movers.

Finding a reliable, trustworthy mover is not always easy. Although the majority of moving companies are honest and reputable, there are fly-by-night movers known for over-charging and dishonesty. I highly recommend calling the Better Business Bureau in your area to check their status. Your Realtor or attorney will recommend a dependable moving company.

Waiting to Close

As closing day approaches, you will be busy packing and preparing for the move. Here are a few matters that will have to be taken care of to make the transition smoother:

The week before

Call your mover – confirm the date and time they will arrive.

Arrange to change the utilities – You will need to call utility companies to have your name removed from the billing and switched over to the new owners. In some areas, readings will need to be taken to close out the account. This is usually done the week before the scheduled closing:

- Electric
- Gas/Oil
- Water
- Cable TV

Several days before

Mail – Stop at the Post Office to arrange for mail to be forwarded to your new address.

Telephone – Call the phone company to transfer or terminate service.

Garbage – Notify your garbage collector of your move.

Newspaper – Have the newspaper delivery service terminated.

Insurance – Notify your homeowner's insurance company that you will be vacating the house. It is wise to tell the insurance agent that you will call *after the closing* to cancel the policy. Closings don't always happen as scheduled, and you must have insurance coverage until the house has changed hands.

The day before

- Call the attorney or closing agent and your Realtor to verify everything is on schedule. You can do this two or three days before if you choose to.
- Gather any documents that you need to bring to the closing.
- Leave garage door openers, appliance warranty paperwork and extra house keys on the kitchen counter for the new owners.

CLOSING DAY

It's finally over.

CLOSING DAY

The Walk-Thru

Prior to the closing, the buyers will walk through the house. It can immediately precede the closing, or take place the day before. The purpose of the walk-thru is for the buyers to be satisfied that nothing has changed since the structural inspection, which is usually the last time they have been inside the house. They will also be checking to ensure that systems are functioning, such as toilets, showers and heat/air conditioning. Essentially, they have the right to expect the house to be in the same condition as when they agreed to purchase it.

Quick Story – A Realtor I know who specializes in distressed and foreclosed properties sold a house in a run-down neighborhood just after a heavy snow fall. The structure was an abandoned "crack house", frequented by drug users in the past. She closed the deal quickly and several weeks later arrived at the house for the walk-thru before the closing. The snow had melted, revealing a corpse in the back yard. Needless to say, the closing was delayed while the police investigated.

The moral of the story is this: It is usually best to remove any dead bodies prior to putting your house on the market.

The role of the seller in the walk-thru is to make sure you are delivering the house to the buyers as promised. The house should be:

Thoroughly Clean

Sweep and vacuum, clean the windows, wipe counters, etc.

Completely Vacant

That means everything must be out, unless they have agreed to buy personal items, such as the refrigerator or any furniture. You cannot make a decision the day before to leave an old sofa, thinking the buyers might want it. When you arrive at the closing, they may demand it be removed and insist that money be held in escrow.

No Damage

Check the house for any damage caused by moving. Even when careful, movers may bump into walls and doors while moving heavy items, causing marks, dents and paint chipping. This must be fixed.

Repair items

The buyers will be checking to confirm that problems you agreed to fix after the structural inspection have been corrected. If you agreed to make a repair, but time has run out, call the Realtor or attorney to offer a financial settlement as an alternative.

Money held in escrow

On occasion, disputes will arise at the closing. It can be a repair that is incomplete or not to the buyer's satisfaction. They may discover something wrong during the walk-thru or personal items that were not removed from the house.

These matters must be settled before the closing can proceed.

A common way to settle disagreements at the closing is for money to be held in escrow until the task is complete. For example, you arranged to give your old pool table to a friend, and left it in the garage. He agreed to pick it up, but forgot about it. The buyers may demand that money be held in escrow until the pool table is picked up. A time frame and money amount are agreed upon, and the money is held in escrow. When the pool table is removed, your money is returned. If any new damage is discovered during the walk-thru, or something is not functioning, the buyers will insist that money be held in escrow until the repair is made, after which the balance of the money will be refunded to you.

The closing

The closing of title normally takes place at the office of an attorney or title company, or sometimes in the real estate office. Be sure to bring the house keys with you to turn over to the buyers, as well as any documents necessary. The buyers usually arrive first, because they have to deal with mortgage documents which can take an hour or longer to sign. Your part of the proceedings will usually take less than an hour. You only have to sign several documents.

The keys to the property are given to the buyers and the closing is complete. The house now belongs to them.

And you breathe a huge sigh of relief.

COLOSSAL MISTAKE

IGNORING YOUR REALTOR'S ADVICE

This could just be the most colossal of all the mistakes in this book. Your Realtor is the greatest asset in your home sale transaction. Yet I continue to be mystified when I hear another story about how a Realtor's advice was ignored.

Realtors have historically been placed into the category of "salesperson." I have never believed the term salesperson was fitting for a Realtor. A Realtor is a salesperson only in the most general sense of the word. The terms "consultant" or "facilitator" are far closer to the actual function of a real estate professional. Managing the transaction is the principal part of a Realtor's job.

Your Realtor has a loyalty to you and a legal duty to you that few other professionals have. When you hire a Realtor, you are employing a consultant who is an expert on the local real estate market and has a very specialized knowledge about marketing and merchandising houses.

So why would you employ a professional consultant who possesses experience and expertise that you don't have and then *not heed* their advice?

When a Realtor says your house is overpriced, refusing to reduce the price is foolish. Realtors don't tell you this to irritate you. Remember you hired her to be candid and give her best advice. She knows you will ultimately get less money for your house if it's overpriced and stays on the market for an extended period of time. The price you **want** to get or **need** to get for the house is absolutely irrelevant. It is worth what someone is willing to pay for it, and not one cent more.

When a Realtor tells you the house should be painted, you will lose money by not painting. This is true of any improvement. Remember, even small investments can pay big dividends, and your Realtor knows exactly what enhancements will return the most money.

If a Realtor makes suggestions about structural concerns, follow them. Your Realtor is only trying to help you avoid needless expense, time-consuming headaches and potential legal predicaments.

A FEW FINAL WORDS

My purpose with this book has been to educate you to become a really smart home seller.

The home sale transaction is full of mistakes waiting to happen. I hope reading this book has minimized the possibility that you will not lose time and money by making one of them.

May all of your real estate transactions be profitable and stress-free!

To contact me:
www.colossalmistakes.com

If you want me to recommend
the best local Realtor for you visit:
www.colossalmistakes.com

COMPILATION OF COLOSSAL MISTAKES

COMPILATION OF COLOSSAL MISTAKES

Here they are, in case you didn't actually read the book, but just need the highlights:

COLOSSAL MISTAKE: Trying to sell your house without a Realtor.

COLOSSAL MISTAKE: Hiring a part-time Realtor.

COLOSSAL MISTAKE: Choosing a Realtor based on a price opinion.

COLOSSAL MISTAKE: Listing your house for sale with a discount broker

COLOSSAL MISTAKE: Not using an Attorney.

COLOSSAL MISTAKE: Choosing an attorney who does not specialize in real estate

COLOSSAL MISTAKE: Setting too high a price

COLOSSAL MISTAKE: Setting too low a price

COLOSSAL MISTAKE: Failing to reduce the price quickly.

COLOSSAL MISTAKE: Ignoring your Realtor's price opinion

COLOSSAL MISTAKE: Selling to a builder without first getting a market analysis.

COLOSSAL MISTAKE: Not doing everything possible to enhance, improve, fix up, beautify, embellish, aggrandize and spruce up your house.

COLOSSAL MISTAKE: Not getting rid of foul odors.

COLOSSAL MISTAKE: Making expensive upgrades that won't increase the value of your house.

COLOSSAL MISTAKE: Making your house difficult to show.

COLOSSAL MISTAKE: Following buyers around the house.

COLOSSAL MISTAKE: Dealing with a buyer not pre-approved for a mortgage.

COLOSSAL MISTAKE: Accepting an offer with a contingency to sell their house.

COLOSSAL MISTAKE: Concealing material defects of the house.

COLOSSAL MISTAKE: Not doing everything possible to settle structural disputes.

COLOSSAL MISTAKE: Making repairs.

COLOSSAL MISTAKE: Not addressing environmental concerns prior to listing your house for sale.

COLOSSAL MISTAKE: Attempting to remove asbestos yourself.

COLOSSAL MISTAKE: Ignoring your Realtor's advice.

OTHER
HELPFUL STUFF

The 1031 Exchange

The following was contributed by Rich Vaill,
Senior Vice President, Excalibur 1031 Group, LLC

The Tax Code Makes It Possible To Exchange Taxes for Profits

Deferring taxes can be an excellent way to preserve your real estate portfolio and leave more wealth to your heirs. For many years, prudent investment property owners have been using Section 1031 of the Internal Revenue Code to save money when they sell an investment property.

Upon the sale of an investment property, this part of the tax code allows a person to make a "delayed exchange," which provides an exchangor with a period of time to locate and close on a replacement property. It is called "delayed" because the replacement property has not been identified prior to the sale of your existing (or relinquished) property. The delayed exchange allows owners of investment property to legally defer state and federal capital gains associated with the sale of that property.

Exchange Periods

The first thing to remember is that the exchange must be completed within 180 days from the close of escrow of the property that was sold. The time on the clock does not begin until the close of escrow on the sold property, but each calendar day is counted, including holidays.

Upon the close of escrow, the taxpayer has 45 days to identify their replacement properties. After the 45 day period, the taxpayer will have an additional 135 days to actually close the transaction, thus completing 180 days. These time period requirements must be strictly followed.

Property Identification

There are basically three rules that apply, and the exchangor must satisfy one of the rules, not all of them. The first rule is called the 3-Property Rule, and this basically states that the maximum number of properties the client may identify is three, without respect to fair market value. The second rule is the 200% rule, which states that any number of properties may be identified as long as the total fair market value does not exceed 200% of the total fair market value of all relinquished properties. The third and final rule is the 95% rule. An Exchangor may identify any number of properties without regard to the combined fair market value, as long as the properties actually acquired amounts to at least 95 percent of the fair market value of all identified properties.

Taxpayers are allowed to change their mind as many times as they wish within the 45 day period. However, once day 45 arrives, whatever property the taxpayer identified last must be used to complete the exchange.

Like – Kind Exchange

The properties exchanged must qualify and be of "like kind." This term refers to the nature of the property, not its grade or quality. Generally, property meets the "like-kind" rule as long as the exchangor's intent is to hold the property as investment or for productive use in a trade or business. Keep in mind, owner occupied residences do not comply with the regulations of a 1031 exchange.

Equal and Up Rule

In a 1031 Exchange, there must be an actual exchange, not just a transfer of property for money only. The Exchangor must acquire replacement property equal to or greater in value than the relinquished property. In addition, the equity in the replacement property must be equal to or greater than the equity in the relinquished property and all net proceeds must be used in acquiring replacement property. Finally, the debt in the replacement property must be equal or greater than the debt on the relinquished property. A seller could pay off the debt prior to closing and thus eliminate this issue.

Qualified Intermediary

In order to complete a delayed exchange, it is necessary to use a disinterested third party to hold funds between the sale of the relinquished property and the purchase of the replacement property. The third party cannot be your attorney, CPA, escrow holder, or real estate broker. Using any of these individuals will disallow the exchange. You will also need to have a series of documents outlining the exchange and they need to be signed by both the seller and buyer of the property.

There are companies that specialize in providing this service and are known as Qualified Intermediaries (QI's), exchange companies, or accommodators. These companies provide clients with experienced professionals dedicated to assisting them with the completion of their exchange. They will provide the necessary documents and will coordinate the transaction with the closing agents and real estate professionals. Often these companies have extensive insurance and banking programs designed to make the exchange safe and efficient.

Next time you plan on selling your investment property, think about the potential of a section 1031 exchange. The savings can be significant and with the assistance of exchange companies, the process is easy.

The information described above is simply a brief overview, and is not intended to provide a complete or comprehensive coverage of Section 1031 of the Internal Revenue Code. All taxpayers should consult with their tax and legal advisors regarding their particular circumstances.

The Excalibur 1031 Group, LLC is a Qualified Intermediary. For more information about 1031 Exchanges, please contact Rich Vaill from the Excalibur 1031 Group, LLC at (877) 644-1031 or rvaill@excalibur1031.com.

Sample marketing plan

SAMPLE MARKETING PLAN

Prepared For: Mr. and Mrs. William Blake
                          505 Central Avenue

Prepared By: Duncan Smythe

Our system approach is designed not just to sell your home, but also to ensure that you obtain the highest possible price with the best possible terms. Full Service involves <u>marketing</u>, <u>merchandising</u>, <u>networking</u> & <u>negotiating</u>. This plan has been carefully customized for your home.

Pricing Strategy: Pricing is a significant part of marketing. Properly positioning your home based on the most recent buyer behavior will be critical to our success. Regularly scheduled market activity analysis will keep you abreast of inventory changes that may affect your position.

Office Notification: The availability of your home will be brought to the immediate attention of all sales associates in our office. This creates a true sense of urgency as the agents contact their existing buyer clients.

Yard Sign: (Optional) With your permission, our distinctive company sign will be placed on the property. This will alert prospective buyers admiring the neighborhood to the availability of your home.

Internet Promotion: While homes are not sold on the Internet, many people contacting our office inquiring about homes for sale come from our Internet exposure. There will be multiple photos, and links to community information. In addition, your home will be featured in:

Realtor.com
OurCompany.com
LocalTownWebsite.com

Office Preview: Scheduled for the first Monday morning following the start of the listing period. The agents from our office will be inspecting the home and providing valuable feedback on our positioning of the property.

Direct Mail: An announcement of the availability of your home will be sent to the immediate neighborhood and to specific target groups.

Multiple Listing Service: The listing of your home will be submitted to the Multiple Listing Service, exposing the property to all Realtor members. Other agents will then have an opportunity to introduce buyers to the property.

Realtor Inspection: A broker "Open House" event will be scheduled for your home. You need not be present. This allows other agents to preview the property for their clients at a prescribed time, eliminating inconvenient appointments through you.

Marketing to Other Realtors: A variety of activities will be acted upon to bring your home to the attention of the top-selling agents. Our company has an internal web site where your home is promoted to the top agents in the company. In addition, a direct mail campaign will be implemented whereby the top 20% of all agents will receive a brochure of your home.

Mortgage Services: Through our company's mortgage group we have the ability to immediately pre–approve prospective buyers of your home. In addition to competitive traditional financing, we can often provide creative alternative financing options for qualified buyers.

Advertising: In addition to our regional buyer's magazine and Internet exposure, you benefit from our national advertising (print, radio and television) as our powerful name recognition is instrumental in developing and maintaining a strong customer base.

Our office also maintains a strong presence in all the major newspaper publications in our area. Your home will be featured in:

The Local Gazette
The Suburban Advertiser
The State Ledger
The Wall Street Journal
The New York Times

Presentation Materials: Prospective buyers viewing your home will have access to an information brochure, school report data, town profile and financing options. The availability of the seller's disclosure statement will also be made known.

Public Open House Event: (Optional) Our office has experienced successful results by advertising that a special property will be available for viewing during a prescribed time on a certain date. The event is advertised and a description of the home provided.

Corporate Relocation: Our company relocation division handles most of the relocation business throughout the country, serving many of America's leading corporations. We are the primary broker for our area to assist in the home search for relocating employees.

Marketing Activity Report: We will provide you with a Marketing Activity Report on a regular basis to keep you informed of market conditions, activity, and the actions we have taken to promote your home.

Negotiating Strategy: Your agent will be at your side to assist with all matters requiring negotiation, including price, terms and conditions of the contract and inspection issues.

Commission Schedule: The marketing fee will be a total of 6% with 3% going to the "selling" office.

Closing the Sale:

>   Contract negotiation
>   Attorney Review
>   Home Inspection
>   Appraisal
>   Pre – Closing tasks
>   Attend closing

Guarantee: *Our commitment that our company and your agent will perform the services stated above as part of the exclusive listing agreement on your property.*

Additional Services: Our Company takes pride in enhancing your entire home selling experience. Ask your agent about other services available.

Week One:

Office Notification	Immediate
Entry into Multiple Listing Service	24 Hours
Direct Notification to Top Area Associates	24 Hours
Presentation Materials (Color brochures)	48 Hours
Office Preview	1st Monday
Broker "Open House"	1st Tuesday after MLS
Internet Promotion	Immediately *Realtor.com* *OurCompany.com*
Local Advertising	Schedule
Other Print Advertising	Schedule
Inter-Office Promotion (Company offices in other towns)	48 Hours
Public "Open House" Event	Schedule
Direct Mail – Target Areas	48 Hours

Seller's estimated closing costs

Real Estate Brokerage Commission $_____
>   Generally 5% - 7% of purchase price

Legal Fee $_____
>   Generally $800 - $1500 depending on the attorney

Realty Transfer Tax $_____
>   Varies by State. Consult your attorney or Realtor.

Mortgage Payoff $_____
>   Balance of mortgage plus interest.

Tax Adjustment $_____
>   Can be a credit or charge to the seller.
>   Seller must pay taxes through closing date.

Utility Adjustments $_____
>   Seller must pay utilities through closing date.
>   Buyer must purchase unused oil in tank, etc.

Removal of Liens $_____
>   Seller must pay off existing liens, including filing
>   fees.

Other Adjustments and Remedial Costs $_____
>   As agreed between the buyer and seller to
>   remediate or repair structural problems.

Thinking of becoming
a Realtor?

Thinking of becoming a Realtor?

So you think you might want to become a Realtor.

Many express an interest in real estate as a career, but few know what's involved. It can be an enjoyable and rewarding career, but there are negative aspects. Between 2000 and 2005, the membership in the National Association of Realtors rose by 300,000 to more than 1.3 million. There is more to being a Realtor than having a driver's license and a clean, respectable car. Let's start with the educational requirements.

Educational Requirements.

Each state has a Real Estate Commission, which is responsible for implementing and enforcing state law and administrative regulations concerning real estate transactions. Every state has different licensing requirements, most mandating some type of schooling. There is usually a state test, which can be difficult, and continuing education. The company you go to work for may have introductory classes and apprenticeships or mentor programs to help you learn the ropes.

In the State of New Jersey, where I work, the basic requirements are:

Minimum age - 18
High school diploma
75 hour real estate licensing course
State Exam

Time Demands

The real estate business can be very time demanding. This is one aspect of the business that can cause aspiring Realtors to lose interest. Realtors almost always work on the weekend. Think about when you bought your home. When did you want to look at houses? Evenings and weekends. Don't count on being with your family all the time. Additionally, a good Realtor is available to customers when needed, not always at a convenient time. I can't count the number of times my phone has rung and I've been forced to skip a meal or been late for a get-together. That is just the nature of this profession. A friend once pointed out, "You can work your own hours". I responded, "That's true, I can work any 50 hours I want to". If you don't care to work a lot of hours including most weekends, consider a different line of work.

Stress

A couple of years ago, The New York Times ran a story listing the Top Ten most stressful occupations. To the surprise of not a single Realtor, we made the list. This job can be very rewarding, but very demanding. More than most jobs, there are a myriad of continuing details.

As a Realtor, you are the manager of the transaction. You are at the fulcrum of each step between every party to the deal. Daily communication between the seller and the buyer, the other Realtor, the home inspector, the attorneys, the appraiser, the mortgage company, the municipal zoning officer, etc. all go through you. You must be fully aware of everything that's happening between all parties to the transaction. More often than not, things do not run smoothly. There are always questions, disagreements, negotiations, and you will be constantly handling requests for information. Any problem or disagreement that arises will precipitate a phone call to you. You are the glue that holds the deal together, and it is common for the Realtor to receive the blame if something goes wrong with the transaction. This generally continues daily for 60 to 90 days until the closing. If you become successful, try balancing five, or even ten transactions at the same time. The life of a Realtor is typically hectic and stressful.

Money

Most Realtors are independent contractors working on a commission. That means you don't get paid until you sell a property and it closes. No weekly salary. No benefits. No health insurance. It is a great advantage to have a spouse who can provide medical coverage.

Outsiders believe Realtors are earning much more than they actually are. The truth is that the nationwide median income of Realtors in 2006 was under $50,000. Your business will build with time, but can never be predicted. It's not uncommon for a Realtor to have a great year, followed by a year in which they earn half of what they did the prior year. Many agents earn NOTHING their first year in the business. Not for a lack of trying, because even with monumental effort, deals may not come together.

QUICK STORY – *Early in my real estate career, I spent seven consecutive weekends showing houses to an engaged couple all around my area. I was calling them nearly every day to inform them of new listings. If I didn't call them, they would call me. I began to feel like a member of their family. They were extremely anxious to find the right house. Then one day I received a call from them. They excitedly announced that they had walked into an open house in another area and immediately bought it. It was difficult for me to share their enthusiasm.*

This has happened to every Realtor I know. The real estate business requires a huge time investment that may not have a positive result. There is not always a lot of loyalty among customers. It is not a job for someone who gets discouraged easily.

A new Realtor should be prepared to earn NO money the first year in business. Be sure you have sufficient funds in the bank to carry you for at least the first year.

Does it sound like I'm trying to dissuade you from entering the real estate profession? I know it may sound that way. I just want you to know exactly what you're facing. I have watched many new people come into the business with unrealistic expectations. It is not a get-rich-quick scheme. It is a business that builds slowly, and requires a lot of hard work.

The Pros of becoming a Realtor

Now that I've painted a dreary picture of life as a Realtor, here are the positives:

Respectable Income – There are many Realtors who earn over $100,000 yearly. Although most are not in this category, it is certainly possible for dedicated agents who are willing to work hard and make the time commitment. Working in the right market area helps, too.

Work Schedule – Realtors make their own schedule. Setting your own appointments is a great convenience. You can usually make yourself available for important events like your kids' ball games, recitals and other activities. It's also a great career choice if you don't want to get up early every day. Customers generally prefer to visit houses in the afternoon or evening hours.

Work Locally – There is something very appealing about working near home. In my market area, most clients are within a 10-15 minute drive. People who commute commonly spend 30-60 minutes traveling each way every day. That really adds up over the course of a year. If I have a break between appointments, I can go home. If I have to be in the office until 6:00, I can be home by 6:10.

Always Active – If the idea of sitting behind a desk from 9 to 5 makes you itch, this is the job for you. You will *never* sit behind a desk for eight straight hours. Your activities and the demands of the job change daily.

Vacation – You are self-employed. You can take vacation any time you want to.

How to contact your Real Estate Commission

REAL ESTATE COMMISSIONS

Here is contact information for the Real Estate Commission in your state:

Alabama

Alabama Real Estate Commission
1201 Carmichael Way
Montgomery, Alabama 36106
334-242-5544
http://www.arec.state.al.us/

Alaska

Alaska Real Estate Commission
Robert B. Atwood Building
550 W. 7th Avenue, Suite 1500
Anchorage, AK 99501
907-269-8197
http://www.dced.state.ak.us/occ/prec.htm

Arizona

Arizona Department of Real Estate
2910 N. 44th Street, Suite 100
Phoenix, AZ 85018
602-468-1414
http://www.re.state.az.us/

Arkansas

Arkansas Real Estate Commission
612 So. Summit Street
Little Rock, AR 72201-4740
501-683-8010
http://www.arkansas.gov/arec/arecweb.html

California

California Department of Real Estate
2201 Broadway
Sacramento, CA 95818-2500
916-227-0864
http://www.dre.ca.gov/

Colorado

Colorado Division of Real Estate
1560 Broadway, Suite 925
Denver, CO 80202
303-894-2166
http://www.dora.state.co.us/real-estate/index.htm

Connecticut

Connecticut Real Estate Commission
Department of Consumer Protection
165 Capitol Avenue
Hartford, Connecticut 06106-1630
860-713-6050
http://www.ct.gov/dcp/cwp/view.asp?a=1624&q=276076

Delaware

Delaware Real Estate Commission
Cannon Building, Suite 203
861 Silver Lake Blvd.
Dover, DE 19904
302-744-4519
http://dpr.delaware.gov/boards/realestate/

Florida

Florida Division of Real Estate
1940 North Monroe Street
Tallahassee, FL 32399-1027
850-487-1395
http://www.myflorida.com/dbpr/re/index.shtml

Georgia

Georgia Real Estate Commission
229 Peachtree St. NE
Suite 1000, International Tower
Atlanta, GA 30303
404-656-3916
http://www.grec.state.ga.us/

Hawaii

Hawaii Real Estate Branch
King Kalakaua Building
335 Merchant Street, Rm. 333
Honolulu, HI 96813
808-586-2643
http://www.hawaii.gov/dcca/areas/real

Idaho

Idaho Real Estate Commission
633 N 4th Street
PO Box 83720
Boise, ID 83720-0077
208-334-3285
http://www.idahorealestatecommission.com/

Illinois

Illinois Bureau of Real Estate Professions
500 E. Monroe, Suite 200
Springfield, IL 62701-1509
877-793-3470
http://www.idfpr.com/dpr/RE/realmain.asp

Indiana

Indiana Real Estate Commission
402 West Washington Street, Room W072
Indianapolis, Indiana 46204
317-234-3009
http://www.in.gov/pla/bandc/estate/

Iowa

Iowa Real Estate Commission
1920 S.E. Hulsizer Road
Ankeny, IA 50021-3941
515-281-5910
http://www.state.ia.us/government/com/prof/sales/home.html

Kansas

Kansas Real Estate Commission
#3 Townsite Plaza, Ste. 200
120 SE 6th Ave
Topeka KS 66603
785-296-3411
http://www.accesskansas.org/krec/

Kentucky

Kentucky Real Estate Commission
10200 Linn Station Road, Suite 201
Louisville, KY 40223
502-429-7250
http://www.krec.ky.gov/

Louisiana

Louisiana Real Estate Commission
P.O. Box 14785
Baton Rouge, LA 70898-4785
225-765-0191
http://www.lrec.state.la.us/

Maine

Maine Real Estate Commission
#35 State House Station
Augusta, Maine 04333-0035
207-624-8515
http://www.maine.gov/pfr/olr/categories/cat38.htm

Maryland

Maryland Real Estate Commission
500 North Calvert Street
Baltimore, MD 21202-3651
410-230-6200
http://www.dllr.state.md.us/license/occprof/recomm.html

Massachusetts

Massachusetts Real Estate Board
239 Causeway Street, Suite 500
Boston, MA 02114
617-727-2373
http://www.mass.gov/dpl/boards/re/

Michigan

Michigan State Board of Real Estate Brokers and Salespersons
P. O. Box 30243
Lansing, MI 48909
517-241-9265
http://www.michigan.gov/cis

Minnesota

Minnesota Department of Commerce
133 East 7th Street
St. Paul, MN 55101
612-296-2488
http://www.state.mn.us/portal/mn/jsp/content.do?subchannel=-
536881389&id=-536881352&agency=Commerce

Mississippi

Mississippi Real Estate Commission
1920 Dunbarton Drive
Jackson, MS 39216-5087
601-987-3969
http://www.mrec.state.ms.us/default.asp

Missouri

Missouri Real Estate Commission
P.O. Box 1339
Jefferson City, MO 65102
314-751-2628
http://pr.mo.gov/realestate.asp

Montana

Montana Board of Realty Regulation
111 N. Jackson
P.O. Box 200513
Helena, MT 59620-0513
406-444-2961
http://mt.gov/dli/bsd/license/bsd_boards/rre_board/board_page.asp

Nebraska

Nebraska Real Estate Commission
1200 N Street, Suite 402
P.O. Box 94667
Lincoln, NE 68509-4667
402-471-2004
http://www.nrec.state.ne.us/

Nevada

Nevada Real Estate Division
2501 E. Sahara
Las Vegas, NV 89158
702-486-4033
http://www.red.state.nv.us/

New Hampshire

New Hampshire Real Estate Commission
State House Annex, Room 434
25 Capitol Street
Concord, New Hampshire 03301
603-271-2701
http://www.state.nh.us/nhrec/

New Jersey

New Jersey Real Estate Commission
20 West State Street, CN-328
Trenton, NJ 08625
609-292-8280
http://www.state.nj.us/dobi/remnu.shtml

New Mexico

New Mexico Real Estate Commission

5200 Oakland Ave. NE, Suite #B
Albuquerque, NM 87113

505-222-9820
http://rld.state.nm.us/b&c/recom/index.htm

New York

New York Office of Real Property Services
84 Holland Ave.
Albany, NY 12208
518-473-2728
http://www.orps.state.ny.us/

North Carolina

North Carolina Real Estate Commission
P.O. Box 17100
Raleigh, NC 27619-7100
919-875-3700
http://www.ncrec.state.nc.us/default.html

North Dakota

North Dakota Real Estate Commission
200 E Main Ave, Ste 204
Bismarck, ND 58502-0727
701-328-9749
http://www.governor.state.nd.us/boards/boards-
query.asp?Board_ID=93

Ohio

Ohio Division of Real Estate
77 South High Street, 20th Floor
Columbus, OH 43266-0547
614-466-4100
http://www.com.state.oh.us/real/

Oklahoma

Oklahoma Real Estate Commission
2401 N.W. 23rd Street, Suite 18
Oklahoma City, Oklahoma 73107
405-521-3387
http://orec.ok.gov/

Oregon

Oregon Real Estate Agency
1177 Center St., N.E.
Salem, OR 97310-2503
503-378-4170

Pennsylvania

Pennsylvania Real Estate Commission
P.O. Box 2649
Harrisburg, PA 17105-2649
717-783-3658
http://www.dos.state.pa.us/

Rhode Island

Rhode Island Department of Business Regulation
233 Richmond St.
Providence, RI 02903
401-222-2246
http://www.dbr.state.ri.us/real_estate.html

South Carolina

South Carolina Real Estate Commission
PO Box 11847
Columbia, S.C. 29211-1847
803-896-4400
http://www.llr.state.sc.us/POL/RealEstateCommission/

South Dakota

South Dakota Real Estate Commission
222 E. Capitol, Suite 101
Pierre, SD 57501-0490
605-773-3600
http://www.state.sd.us/sdrec/

Tennessee

Tennessee Real Estate Commission
500 James Robertson Parkway
Nashville, TN 37243-1151
800-342-4031
http://www.state.tn.us/commerce/boards/trec/

Texas

Texas Real Estate Commission
P.O. Box 12188
Austin, TX 78711-2188
512-459-6544
http://www.trec.state.tx.us/

Utah

Utah Division of Real Estate
P.O. Box 146711
Salt Lake City, UT 84114-6711
801-530-6747
http://realestate.utah.gov/

Vermont

Vermont Real Estate Commission
109 State Street
Montpelier, VT 05609-1106
802-828-3228

Virginia

Virginia Department of Professional and Occupational Regulation
3600 West Broad Street
Richmond, VA 23230
804-367-8552
http://www.state.va.us/dpor/reb_main

Washington

Washington Department of Licensing
Real Estate Program
P.O. Box 9015
Olympia, WA 98507
360-664-6488
http://www.dol.wa.gov/realestate/refront.htm

West Virginia

West Virginia Real Estate Commission
300 Capitol Street, Suite 400
Charleston, WV 25301
304-558-3555
http://www.wvrec.org/

Wisconsin

Wisconsin Department of Regulation & Licensing
Office of Examinations - Real Estate
P.O. Box 8935
Madison, WI 53708
608-266-2112
http://drl.wi.gov/index.htm

Wyoming

Wyoming Real Estate Commission
2020 Carey Avenue, Suite 702
Cheyenne, Wyoming 82002-0180
307-777-7141
http://realestate.state.wy.us/

U.S. Virgin Islands

Virgin Islands Board of Real Estate Commission
Golden Rock Shopping Center,
Christiansted, St. Croix, VI 00822
340-773-2226
http://www.dlca.gov.vi/recrequirements.htm

Washington, D.C.

Washington, D.C. Board of Real Estate
1350 Pennsylvania Avenue, NW
Washington, DC 20004
202-442-4344
http://dcra.dc.gov/dcra/cwp/view,a,1342,q,600757,dcraNav_GID,16
97,dcraNav,%7C33466%7C.asp

Glossary of
Real Estate Terms

.

GLOSSARY OF REAL ESTATE TERMS

A

Amenity: a feature of the home or property that serves as a benefit to the buyer but that is not necessary to its use; may be natural (like location, woods, water) or man-made (like a swimming pool or garden).

Amortization: repayment of a mortgage loan through monthly installments of principal and interest; the monthly payment amount is based on a schedule that will allow you to own your home at the end of a specific time period (for example, 15 or 30 years).

Annual Percentage Rate (APR): calculated by using a standard formula, the APR shows the cost of a loan; expressed as a yearly interest rate, it includes the interest, points, mortgage insurance, and other fees associated with the loan.

Application: the first step in the official loan approval process; this form is used to record important information about the potential borrower necessary to the underwriting process.

Appraisal: a document that gives an estimate of a property's fair market value; an appraisal is generally required by a lender before loan approval to ensure that the mortgage loan amount is not more than the value of the property.

Appraiser: a qualified individual who uses his or her experience and knowledge to prepare the appraisal estimate.

ARM: Adjustable Rate Mortgage; a mortgage loan subject to changes in interest rates; when rates change, ARM monthly payments increase or decrease at intervals determined by the lender; the change in monthly payment amount, however, is usually subject to a cap.

Assessor: a government official who is responsible for determining the value of a property for the purpose of taxation.

Assumable mortgage: a mortgage that can be transferred from a seller to a buyer; once the loan is assumed by the buyer the seller is no longer responsible for repaying it; there may be a fee and/or a credit package involved in the transfer of an assumable mortgage.

B

Balloon Mortgage: a mortgage that typically offers low rates for an initial period of time (usually 5, 7, or 10) years; after that time period elapses, the balance is due or is refinanced by the borrower.

Bankruptcy: a federal law whereby a person's assets are turned over to a trustee and used to pay off outstanding debts; this usually occurs when someone owes more than they have the ability to repay.

Borrower: a person who has been approved to receive a loan and is then obligated to repay it and any additional fees according to the loan terms.

Building code: based on agreed upon safety standards within a specific area, a building code is a regulation that determines the design, construction, and materials used in the building.

Budget: a detailed record of all income earned and spent during a specific period of time.

C

Cap: a limit, such as that placed on an adjustable rate mortgage, on how much a monthly payment or interest rate can increase or decrease.

Cash reserves: a cash amount sometimes required to be held in reserve in addition to the down payment and closing costs; the amount is determined by the lender.

Certificate of title: a document provided by a qualified source (such as a title company) that shows the property legally belongs to the current owner; before the title is transferred at closing, it should be clear and free of all liens or other claims.

Closing: also known as settlement, this is the time at which the property is formally sold and transferred from the seller to the buyer; it is at this time that the borrower takes on the loan obligation and receives title from the seller.

Closing costs: customary costs above and beyond the sale price of the property that must be paid to cover the transfer of ownership at closing; these costs generally vary by geographic location and are typically detailed to the borrower after submission of a loan application.

Commission: an amount, usually a percentage of the property sales price that is collected by a real estate professional as a fee for negotiating the transaction.

Condominium: a form of ownership in which individuals purchase and own a unit of housing in a multi-unit complex; the owner also shares financial responsibility for common areas.

Conventional loan: a private sector loan, one that is not guaranteed or insured by the U.S. government.

Cooperative (Co-op): residents purchase stock in a cooperative corporation that owns a structure; each stockholder is then entitled to live in a specific unit of the structure and is responsible for paying a portion of the loan.

Credit history: history of an individual's debt payment; lenders use this information to gouge a potential borrower's ability to repay a loan.

Credit report: a record that lists all past and present debts and the timeliness of their repayment; it documents an individual's credit history.

Credit bureau score: a number representing the possibility a borrower may default; it is based upon credit history and is used to determine ability to qualify for a mortgage loan.

D

Debt-to-income ratio: a comparison of gross income to housing and non-housing expenses; with the FHA, the monthly mortgage payment should be no more than 29% of monthly gross income (before taxes) and the mortgage payment combined with non-housing debts should not exceed 41% of income.

Deed: the document that transfers ownership of a property.

Deed-in-lieu: to avoid foreclosure ("in lieu" of foreclosure), a deed is given to the lender to fulfill the obligation to repay the debt; this process doesn't allow the borrower to remain in the house but helps avoid the costs, time, and effort associated with foreclosure.

Default: the inability to pay monthly mortgage payments in a timely manner or to otherwise meet the mortgage terms.

Delinquency: failure of a borrower to make timely mortgage payments under a loan agreement.

Discount point: normally paid at closing and generally calculated to be equivalent to 1% of the total loan amount, discount points are paid to reduce the interest rate on a loan.

Down payment: the portion of a home's purchase price that is paid in cash and is not part of the mortgage loan.

E

Earnest money: money put down by a potential buyer to show that he or she is serious about purchasing the home; it becomes part of the down payment if the offer is accepted, is returned if the offer is rejected, or is forfeited if the buyer pulls out of the deal.

Equity: an owner's financial interest in a property; calculated by subtracting the amount still owed on the mortgage loan(s) from the fair market value of the property.

Escrow account: a separate account into which the lender puts a portion of each monthly mortgage payment; an escrow account provides the funds needed for such expenses as property taxes, homeowners insurance, mortgage insurance, etc.

F

Fair Housing Act: a law that prohibits discrimination in all facets of the home buying process on the basis of race, color, national origin, religion, sex, familial status, or disability.

Fair market value: the hypothetical price that a willing buyer and seller will agree upon when they are acting freely, carefully, and with complete knowledge of the situation.

Fannie Mae: Federal National Mortgage Association (FNMA); a federally-chartered enterprise owned by private stockholders that purchases residential mortgages and converts them into securities for sale to investors; by purchasing mortgages, Fannie Mae supplies funds that lenders may loan to potential homebuyers.

FHA: Federal Housing Administration; established in 1934 to advance homeownership opportunities for all Americans; assists homebuyers by providing mortgage insurance to lenders to cover most losses that may occur when a borrower defaults; this encourages lenders to make loans to borrowers who might not qualify for conventional mortgages.

Fixed-rate mortgage: a mortgage with payments that remain the same throughout the life of the loan because the interest rate and other terms are fixed and do not change.

Flood insurance: insurance that protects homeowners against losses from a flood; if a home is located in a flood plain; the lender will require flood insurance before approving a loan.

Foreclosure: a legal process in which mortgaged property is sold to pay the loan of the defaulting borrower.

Freddie Mac: Federal Home Loan Mortgage Corporation (FHLM); a federally chartered corporation that purchases residential mortgages, securitizes them, and sells them to investors; this provides lenders with funds for new homebuyers.

G

Good faith estimate: an estimate of all closing fees including prepaid and escrow items as well as lender charges; must be given to the borrower within three days after submission of a loan application.

H

Home inspection: an examination of the structure and mechanical systems to determine a home's safety; makes the potential homebuyer aware of any repairs that may be needed.

Home warranty: offers protection for mechanical systems and attached appliances against unexpected repairs not covered by homeowner's insurance; coverage extends over a specific time period and does not cover the home's structure.

Homeowner's insurance: an insurance policy that combines protection against damage to a dwelling and its contents with protection against claims of negligence or inappropriate action that result in someone's injury or property damage.

Housing counseling agency: provides counseling and assistance to individuals on a variety of issues, including loan default, fair housing, and home buying.

HUD: the U.S. Department of Housing and Urban Development; established in 1965, HUD works to create a decent home and suitable living environment for all Americans; it does this by addressing housing needs, improving and developing American communities, and enforcing fair housing laws.

HUD1 Statement: also known as the "settlement sheet," it itemizes all closing costs; must be given to the borrower at or before closing.

HVAC: Heating, Ventilation and Air Conditioning; a home's heating and cooling system.

I

Index: a measurement used by lenders to determine changes to the interest rate charged on an adjustable rate mortgage.

Inflation: the number of dollars in circulation exceeds the amount of goods and services available for purchase; inflation results in a decrease in the dollar's value.

Interest: a fee charged for the use of money.

Interest rate: the amount of interest charged on a monthly loan payment; usually expressed as a percentage.

Insurance: protection against a specific loss over a period of time that is secured by the payment of a regularly scheduled premium.

J

Judgment: a legal decision; when requiring debt repayment, a judgment may include a property lien that secures the creditor's claim by providing a collateral source.

L

Lease purchase: assists low to moderate-income homebuyers in purchasing a home by allowing them to lease a home with an option to buy; the rent payment is made up of the monthly rental payment plus an additional amount that is credited to an account for use as a down payment.

Lien: a legal claim against property that must be satisfied when the property is sold.

Loan: money borrowed that is usually repaid with interest.

Loan fraud: purposely giving incorrect information on a loan application in order to better qualify for a loan; may result in civil liability or criminal penalties.

Loan-to-value (LTV) ratio: a percentage calculated by dividing the amount borrowed by the price or appraised value of the home to be purchased; the higher the LTV, the less cash a borrower is required to pay as down payment.

Lock-in: since interest rates can change frequently, many lenders offer an interest rate lock-in that guarantees a specific interest rate if the loan is closed within a specific time.

Loss mitigation: a process to avoid foreclosure; the lender tries to help a borrower who has been unable to make loan payments and is in danger of defaulting on his or her loan

M

Margin: an amount the lender adds to an index to determine the interest rate on an adjustable rate mortgage.

Mortgage: a lien on the property that secures the promise to repay a loan.

Mortgage banker: a company that originates loans and resells them to secondary mortgage lenders like Fannie Mae or Freddie Mac.

Mortgage broker: a firm that originates and processes loans for a number of lenders.

Mortgage insurance: a policy that protects lenders against some or most of the losses that can occur when a borrower defaults on a mortgage loan; mortgage insurance is required primarily for borrowers with a down payment of less than 20% of the home's purchase price.

Mortgage insurance premium (MIP): a monthly payment, usually part of the mortgage payment, paid by a borrower for mortgage insurance.

Mortgage Modification: a loss mitigation option that allows a borrower to refinance and/or extend the term of the mortgage loan and thus reduce the monthly payments.

O

Offer: indication by a potential buyer of a willingness to purchase a home at a specific price; generally put forth in writing.

Origination: the process of preparing, submitting, and evaluating a loan application; generally includes a credit check, verification of employment, and a property appraisal.

Origination fee: the charge for originating a loan; is usually calculated in the form of points and paid at closing.

P

PITI: Principal, Interest, Taxes, and Insurance - the four elements of a monthly mortgage payment; payments of principal and interest go directly towards repaying the loan while the portion that covers taxes and insurance (homeowner's and mortgage, if applicable) goes into an escrow account to cover the fees when they are due.

PMI: Private Mortgage Insurance; privately-owned companies that offer standard and special affordable mortgage insurance programs for qualified borrowers with down payments of less than 20% of a purchase price.

Pre-approve: lender commits to lend to a potential borrower; commitment remains as long as the borrower still meets the qualification requirements at the time of purchase.

Pre-foreclosure sale: allows a defaulting borrower to sell the mortgaged property to satisfy the loan and avoid foreclosure.

Pre-qualify: a lender informally determines the maximum amount an individual is eligible to borrow.

Premium: an amount paid on a regular schedule by a policyholder that maintains insurance coverage.

Prepayment: payment of the mortgage loan before the scheduled due date.

Principal: the amount borrowed from a lender; doesn't include interest or additional fees.

R

Radon: a radioactive gas found in some homes that, if occurring in strong enough concentrations, can cause health problems.

Real estate agent: an individual who is licensed to negotiate and arrange real estate sales; works for a real estate broker.

REALTOR: a real estate agent or broker who is a member of the NATIONAL ASSOCIATION OF REALTORS, and its local and state associations.

Refinancing: paying off one loan by obtaining another; refinancing is generally done to secure better loan terms (like a lower interest rate).

RESPA: Real Estate Settlement Procedures Act; a law protecting consumers from abuses during the residential real estate purchase and loan process by requiring lenders to disclose all settlement costs, practices, and relationships.

S

Seller paid closing costs: adding closing costs to the purchase price to reduce out-of-pocket expenses for the buyer.

Settlement: another name for closing.

Subordinate: to place in a rank of lesser importance or to make one claim secondary to another.

Survey: a property diagram that indicates legal boundaries, easements, encroachments, rights of way, improvement locations, etc.

Sweat equity: using labor to build or improve a property as part of the down payment.

T U V

Title insurance: insurance that protects the lender against any claims that arise from disputes about ownership of the property; also available for homebuyers.

Title search: a check of public records to be sure that the seller is the recognized owner of the real estate and that there are no unsettled liens or other claims against the property.

Truth-in-Lending: a federal law obligating a lender to give full written disclosure of all fees, terms, and conditions associated with the loan initial period and then adjusts to another rate that lasts for the term of the loan.

Underwriting: the process of analyzing a loan application to determine the amount of risk involved in making the loan; it includes a review of the potential borrower's credit history and a judgment of the property value.

VA: Department of Veterans Affairs: a federal agency that guarantees loans made to veterans; similar to mortgage insurance, a loan guarantee protects lenders against loss that may result from a borrower default.

To contact me:
www.colossalmistakes.com

If you want me to recommend
the best local Realtor for you visit:
www.colossalmistakes.com

LaVergne, TN USA
18 August 2009
155050LV00014B/228/P